Meredith Stein, David S. Linthicum
Unlocking the Power of the Cloud

Meredith Stein, David S. Linthicum

Unlocking the Power of the Cloud

—

Governance, Artificial Intelligence, Risk Management, Value

DE GRUYTER

ISBN 978-3-11-161710-7
e-ISBN (PDF) 978-3-11-161745-9
e-ISBN (EPUB) 978-3-11-161820-3

Library of Congress Control Number: 2025941375

Bibliographic information published by the Deutsche Nationalbibliothek
The Deutsche Nationalbibliothek lists this publication in the Deutsche Nationalbibliografie;
detailed bibliographic data are available on the internet at http://dnb.dnb.de.

www.degruyter.com
Questions about General Product Safety Regulation:
productsafety@degruyterbrill.com

This book is dedicated to the memory of Steven Mezzio (1957–2025) and Vincent Campitelli (1937–2022). Their wisdom and passion for cloud governance continue to echo through these pages.

This book is also dedicated to the memory of Ronald Linthicum (1939–2014). David's accomplishments were made with Ronald's encouragement and guidance.

Foreword

In every era of technological transformation, there comes a time when optimism outpaces preparedness. Today, as organizations race toward the promise of the AI-enabled cloud, many find themselves caught between the limitless potential and the sobering complexity of modern digital ecosystems. This book, *Unlocking the Power of the Cloud*, is a timely and essential compass for navigating that terrain. It doesn't simply celebrate the cloud's possibilities—it demands that we confront its realities.

I have spent decades observing, building, and advising on enterprise technologies. And never before have I seen such profound shifts in the way we think about value, risk, governance, and accountability as I have with the intersection of cloud computing and artificial intelligence. We've entered a period where the cloud is no longer just an IT infrastructure decision. It is now a board-level conversation, a strategic differentiator, and a source of competitive risk—all at once.

Meredith Stein and David Linthicum understand this intersection deeply. They know that the cloud's allure—cost savings, scalability, innovation—is real but not guaranteed. They also recognize that cloud adoption isn't a destination; it's a perpetual journey, shaped by evolving technologies, shifting regulatory landscapes, and human factors. This is not a how-to manual. It's something much more important: a governance framework for the age of disruption.

One of the book's core strengths lies in its refusal to reduce cloud governance to technical checklists. Instead, Stein and Linthicum examine cloud transformation as a "wicked problem"—one that defies simple definitions, clear answers, or linear solutions. They call on leaders to grapple with organizational culture, cross-functional accountability, and long-term strategy, not just cloud vendors and architecture. The book challenges decision-makers to ask tougher questions and to develop adaptive, context-aware governance mechanisms.

It's also refreshing to see how the authors confront the mythology of the cloud. Chapter by chapter, they deconstruct the idea of a seamless, utopian future powered by cloud and AI. They offer instead a more balanced view: one where real gains are possible—but only with intentional governance, active risk management, and sustained investment in people, process, and policy. They name the elephants in the room: data breaches, unaccountable shared responsibilities, overhyped vendor promises, and the environmental consequences of digital infrastructure. In doing so, they provide a voice of reason in a sea of marketing hyperbole.

This book's structure reflects its core belief that cloud governance is a living ecosystem. Beginning with foundational principles and moving through performance, compliance, cybersecurity, and board oversight, Stein and Linthicum guide readers through a comprehensive framework. Their "Cloud Governance House" metaphor elegantly organizes the moving parts of cloud strategy, showing how each function—from audit to change management—must work together under one roof. It is a model not just for IT leaders, but for C-suites and directors who need to align digital ambition with fiduciary duty.

Another reason this book stands out is its focus on actionable insight. Every chapter ends with a "Call to Action"—a thoughtful set of steps that organizations can begin applying today. Whether it's conducting a cloud security audit, mapping shared responsibility models, or building an inventory of cloud assets, these actions are practical, grounded, and essential.

Moreover, the authors are unafraid to look to the future. They explore emergent technologies like Quantum Computing, Agentic AI, and Cloud Gaming—not as novelties, but as inevitable forces reshaping risk, regulation, and enterprise architecture. Their analysis of sustainability, cyber insurance gaps, and the board's digital literacy is especially prescient. These are not issues we can defer; they are already affecting how organizations are judged by regulators, investors, and customers.

It's important to note that this book is not just for technologists. It speaks to a much wider audience: boards of directors, CFOs, compliance officers, HR leaders, and strategists. In an age when cloud and AI are inseparable from enterprise governance, this is the kind of resource that every cross-functional leadership team should read together. It brings shared language, shared understanding, and—perhaps most importantly—shared accountability.

In closing, *Unlocking the Power of the Cloud* delivers what the title promises, but with a crucial distinction: it makes clear that power is not granted automatically by technology. Power must be unlocked through responsible stewardship, intentional governance, and an unflinching look at both the promises and the perils of the digital age.

If your organization is navigating cloud transformation, this book will be a trusted guide. If you are responsible for ensuring that transformation is aligned with your mission, values, and obligations—this book may just be indispensable.

Jo Peterson
Vice President Cloud, Security and AI-Clarify360 and Chief Analyst
ClearTech Research

Contents

Foreword —— VII

Part I: **The Basics of Cloud Governance and AI-Enablement**

Chapter 1
The Utopian Promises of the Cloud and the AI-Driven Future —— 3

Chapter 2
The Dark Side of the Cloud —— 16

Chapter 3
The Basics of Cloud Computing —— 22

Part II: **A Look at the Context of Cloud Computing and AI**

Chapter 4
Cloud Strategy and Performance —— 35

Chapter 5
Cloud-Driven Change Management and Learning —— 49

Part III: **Governance Disrupted and Transformed by the Cloud**

Chapter 6
Sharing Cloud Governance Responsibilities and Integrating the Cloud with Enterprise Risk Management —— 65

Chapter 7
Security, Trust, and the Cloud —— 82

Chapter 8
Compliance and the Cloud —— 96

Chapter 9
Audit, Assurance, and the Cloud —— 107

Chapter 10
The Board of Directors: Asking the Right Questions about AI and the Cloud ⸺ 114

Notes ⸺ 123

About the Authors ⸺ 135

List of Figures ⸺ 137

List of Tables ⸺ 139

List of Boxes ⸺ 141

Index ⸺ 143

Part I: **The Basics of Cloud Governance and AI-Enablement**

Chapter 1
The Utopian Promises of the Cloud and the AI-Driven Future

Introduction

The utopian promises of cloud computing, compounded by the chaos of large-scale deployment and the resulting organizational upheaval, have profound and far-reaching governance implications. The chaos of the cloud is a *wicked problem* that creates confusion, perplexity, and risk at various points during a cloud journey. This book will explore how an organization can leverage cloud governance to moderate the extremes, striving to attain the achievable promises of the cloud, on the one hand, and successfully navigating and governing the chaos of the cloud on the other hand.

Utopian Promises vs Realities of Cloud

Don't celebrate promises, and don't fear threats.[2]
– Sicilian Proverb

The Oxford Learner's Dictionary defines utopia as "an imaginary place or state in which everything is perfect." Ernst Bloch, author of The Principle of Hope, suggests that imagining the achievement of utopian-conditions is an important catalyst for change. In the context of the cloud, organizations have universally embraced the promises and are willing to digitally transform to achieve a cloud-driven *utopia*.

Cloud vendors, academics, influencers, and media have contributed to defining and signaling the wide range of transformational benefits available through the cloud. That is, compelling promises of ideal performance, innovation, productivity, cost savings, and much more. Table 1.1 presents examples of such utopian-promises of the cloud.

Table 1.1: Examples of Utopian Promises of the Cloud. Source: Authors.

Categories of the Utopian Promises of the AI-Enabled Cloud
Substantial Cost Reduction | Significant Return on Investment (ROI)
– Lowers capital investments, in-house hardware, software, and IT maintenance – Facilitates increased revenue through innovation and improved customer engagement – Rapidly automates manual processes and enables innovation
Sweeping, Accelerated Gains in Productivity, Efficiency, Innovation, Customer Service
– Enables productive and efficient Democratized IT employees who can collaborate and access data in the cloud – Provides access to cutting edge technologies because of the AI-enabled cloud that can transform IT-capacity (e.g., data storage, IT scaling opportunities, quantum computing)
Reduced Risk | Improved IT Governance
– Enhances compliance with regulatory guidance by leveraging AI – Reduces risk to security with utilization of AI to respond to cyber threats – Decreases carbon footprint

McKinsey found, and the authors agree, that "the value cloud generates from enabling businesses to innovate is worth more than five times what is possible by simply reducing IT costs." See the call out box for a cloud governance success story about a fictious organization that migrated their legacy systems to the cloud.

As the cloud enters a more mature phase and Artificial Intelligence is the most significant technological disruption in decades, an essential question emerges, *Does the cloud deliver on its utopian promises?* It depends.

As with any disruptive and transformational change undertaken by an organization, the level of success depends on a range of complex variables. One variable influencing cloud success is the inherent and inevitable chaos of the cloud. Ernst Bloch stated that "Utopias are seen as impossible."[3] This perspective seems reasonably relevant to the cloud. Some organizations expect to achieve the *utopian promises* of the cloud but fall short because of the inherent *chaos* of the cloud. The Cambridge Dictionary defines chaos as "A state of total confusion with no order."[4]

Is chaos a reality of the cloud? According to Gartner, the following gaps have emerged between the cloud's promises and the chaotic-reality of an organization's cloud journey. Gartner identified the gaps between:

– An organization's aspirations and the ability of in-house staff to execute
– Expected gains from cloud versus the reality of what cloud can deliver
– An organization's business strategy and its cloud strategy
– Existing and required operating model, or the existing and required foundational practices such as governance, "compliance and security"[5]

Table 1.2 presents the authors' list of the chaotic realities of the cloud.

Table 1.2: Top 25 List of the Chaotic Realities of the Cloud, Source: Authors.

Chaos of the Cloud – Top 25 (random order)
1. Incoherent cloud strategy
2. Unbridled vendor activities with organization assets
3. Overreliance on one CSP vendor (concentration risk)
4. Haphazard controls over the extended enterprise
5. Lack of accountability for respective cloud-shared responsibilities
6. No one is in charge of the cloud – bifurcated cloud leadership in the organization
7. Ungoverned workarounds and reengineering needs
8. AI/cloud washing and upselling/overselling by vendors
9. Lack of a skilled AI/cloud-enabled workforce to execute the strategy
10. Increasingly complex data governance
11. Ineffective incident response and inability to investigate root causes of cloud breach
12. Failure to address poor configuration settings resulting in increased cybersecurity risk
13. Unaware of scope, frequency of cyber-threats, and unsuccessful attacks and breaches
14. Intellectual property loss due to data leakage through GenAI
15. Unsanctioned shadow IT and a lack of a reliable, real-time cloud asset inventory
16. Understatement of cloud costs with little consideration for change management, training, cyber insurance, business interruption costs, crisis management costs, and ransomware attacks
17. Introduction of malicious code that compromises GenAI data integrity
18. Pressure to rapidly adopt the cloud before prepared to do so causing success to take longer than expected
19. Fragmented AI solutions creating increased vulnerabilities
20. Rapidly shifting regulatory requirements that differ across geographic jurisdictions and a misalignment with organization AI/cloud-related policies
21. Unknown gaps between liability insurance policies and cyber insurance policies
22. Customer loyalty challenged by cloud breaches and service downtime
23. Growing pressure for board members to be more AI/cloud literate
24. CSP security policies and priorities not aligned with organization policies
25. Convoluted and complicated SLA and CSP contracts

Organizations strive to capitalize on the compelling promises of the cloud. At the same time, failing to recognize and control the chaotic realities of the cloud creates risks to strategy, performance, and cloud governance. An organization's journey towards cloud adoption will not be a straight line; the path will be filled with twists and turns – risks and opportunities. Cloud governance plays a crucial role *moderating* the extremes, striving to attain the achievable promises of the cloud, on the one hand, and successfully navigating and governing the chaos of the cloud on the other hand.

Is the Cloud a Wicked Problem?

> We cannot solve our problems with the same
> thinking we used when we created them.[6]
> – Albert Einstein, Mathematician and Physicist

Wicked problems differ from ordinary problems as,

> Wicked problems often crop up when organizations have to face constant change or unprec-
> edented challenges. They occur in a social context; the greater the disagreement among
> stakeholders, the more wicked the problem. In fact, it's the social complexity of wicked
> problems as much as their technical difficulties that make them tough to manage. Not all
> problems are wicked; confusion, discord, and lack of progress are telltale signs that an issue
> might be wicked.[7]

For this cloud governance book, the term "wicked" refers to Horst Rittel's formal
definition of a problem that is difficult to describe, has many root causes, and has
no correct answer.[8] It is not the definition for malicious intent or moral wrongdo-
ing. In a business strategy context, the Harvard Business Review identified five
common characteristics of a wicked problem.
1. The problem involves many stakeholders with different values and priorities.
2. The issue's roots are complex and tangled.
3. The problem is difficult to come to grips with and changes with every attempt
    to address it.
4. The challenge has no precedent.
5. There's nothing to indicate the right answer to the problem.[9]

How an organization goes about governing a wicked problem may differ in some
important ways as compared to an ordinary or difficult problem. This book explores the question, *Is the cloud a wicked problem? What do you think?*

Cloud Governance Ecosystem

> The first law of ecology is that everything is related to everything else.[10]
> – Barry Commoner, Biologist and Educator

This book focuses on cloud governance concepts and real-world practices. Table 1.3
presents the touchstone definition of cloud governance selected for this book.

This definition captures the business-side and the IT-side of cloud strategy
and, therefore, corporate and cloud governance. Moreover, this definition inte-
grates some of the crucial enablers of effective cloud governance. For instance,

Table 1.3: Definition of Cloud Governance. Source: Thuraisingham.[11]

Definition of Cloud Governance
Cloud computing governance is a view of IT governance focused on accountability, defining decision rights and balancing benefit or value, risk, and resources in an environment embracing cloud computing.
Cloud computing governance creates business-driven policies and principles that establish the appropriate degree of investments and control around the lifecycle process for cloud computing services.

accountability; responsibility (e.g., policies); strategy (e.g., value); risk management, environmental and IT context influences; fit-for-purpose (e.g., adequate resources); and stakeholder trust.

Leveraging this definition of cloud governance as a springboard, this book created a high-level conceptualization of a *cloud governance ecosystem*. The topics in each chapter of this book represent the individual and interconnected components of a cloud governance ecosystem. Figure 1.1 visually depicts the relationships amongst the cloud governance ecosystem components in a Cloud Governance House.

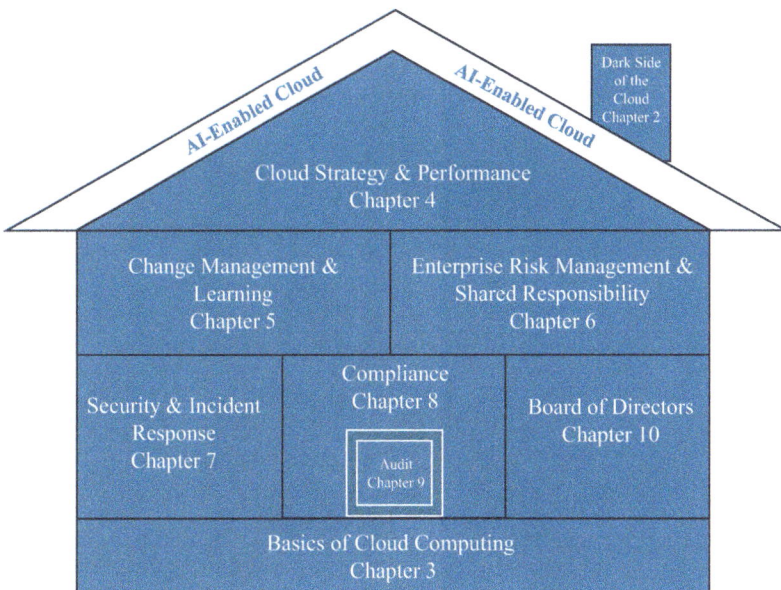

Figure 1.1: Cloud Governance House: A Perspective on the Cloud Governance Ecosystem. Source: Authors.

The roof of the Cloud Governance House is the organization's strategy (e.g., the interrelated business strategy aligned with the IT strategy, the AI-enabled cloud strategy, and performance). The rooms of the house are the cloud-shared responsibility model and the organizational governance functions (e.g., the Board, compliance, audit, etc.). The Cloud Governance House is based on the operating context defined by DePietro et al.'s Technological, Organizational, and Environmental (TOE) framework.[12]

The authors believe that an organization is highly sensitive to the *context* that it operates in. Table 1.4 uses the TOE framework to explore the integration of *context* on cloud governance.

Table 1.4: Variables of TOE Context Framework to Consider During Cloud Adoption to Limit Chaos. Source: Authors.

TOE Framework[13]	Cloud Success Depends On . . .
Technological Context Represents the internal and external technologies related to the firm	1. Maturity and resiliency of cloud governance 2. Infrastructure fit for cloud purpose 3. Integrating the AI-enabled cloud into existing IT governance protocols 4. Risk appetite 5. Incident response capabilities 6. Enabling digital transformation 7. Governing remote technology 8. Data ethics and data governance 9. Legacy system limitations
Organizational Context Relates to the resources and the characteristics of the firm	1. Alignment of organizational strategy with cloud strategy 2. Alignment of organizational governance with cloud governance 3. Oversight of vendor performance 4. Knowledge of the location of cloud assets 5. Compliance with global regulations across geographies 6. Criteria for vendor selection 7. Top-down change management efforts 8. Ability to transform the in-house IT function and create an AI/cloud-enabled workforce 9. Role of the CIO as the business savvy technologist

Table 1.4 (continued)

TOE Framework	Cloud Success Depends On . . .
Environmental Context Refers to the arena in which a firm conducts its business	1. Receptiveness to innovate and explore with Quantum and Edge Computing, AI, Metaverse 2. Due diligence in assessing CSP capabilities 3. Importance of the Cloud Shared Responsibility Model 4. High-profile cyber-attacks at other organizations 5. Lessons learned from good practices at other organizations 6. New and emerging global AI regulations 7. Competition for AI-enabled cloud talent 8. Competitive landscape of cloud vendors 9. Environmental sustainability impact of the cloud

The authors believe that this context substantially influences the success and failure of innovative cloud and AI initiatives that are disruptive and transformational.

What Does the AI-Driven Future Hold for the Cloud?

The future depends on what you do today.[14]
– Mahatma Gandhi, Indian leader and Social Activist

The World Economic Forum surveyed 1,000 global employers, representing more than 14 million workers across 22 industries from around the world, and published the *2025 Future of Jobs Report*, that stated,

Broadening digital access is expected to be the most transformative trend – both across technology-related trends and overall – with 60% of employers expecting it to transform their business by 2030. Advancements in technologies, particularly AI and information processing (86%); robotics and automation (58%); and energy generation, storage and distribution (41%), are also expected to be transformative. These trends are expected to have a divergent effect on jobs, driving both the fastest-growing and fastest-declining roles, and fueling demand for technology-related skills, including AI and big data, networks and cybersecurity and technological literacy.[15]

Organizations and CSPs are already seizing the opportunities to leverage AI-enabled cloud technologies and applications. Such technologies include Quantum Computing, Agentic AI, Cloud Gaming, and the Internet of Things (IoT).

Quantum Computing

McKinsey defines quantum computing as "a new approach to calculation that uses principles of fundamental physics to solve extremely complex problems very quickly."[16] Statista projects the market revenue has the potential to amount to USD 93 billion by 2040.[17] Table 1.5 presents a summary of quantum computing use cases.

Table 1.5: Example Use Cases for Quantum Computing.[18,19,20]

Industry	Quantum Computing Example Use Cases
Healthcare	Examine of digital models to study temperature, metabolism, circulation
Financial	Analyze transaction data for unusual activity and potential fraud
Insurance	Predict weather for climate models
Logistics	Optimize delivery routes
Oil & Gas	Identify natural resources
Public Sector	Predict seismic disruptions such volcanos and earthquakes

The authors think that a medium-sized organization is several years away from achieving a return on investment from quantum computing. Quantum computing introduces unique governance challenges for cloud environments. Cloud governance for quantum computing requires attention of emerging quantum regulations. For example, countries are:

- developing cryptography standards to protect current encryption methods and critical infrastructure that could be vulnerable to quantum attacks
- developing policies to classify quantum technologies as critical to national security to limit foreign investment or ownership of quantum companies and restrict international collaborations
- examining how laws should be updated to protect consumer data and address quantum computing's ability to process and analyze large datasets

Quantum computing also requires management's attention to security protocols for quantum key distribution and specialized access controls that consider the unique nature of quantum information processing. Quantum key distribution protocols necessitate new governance frameworks to verify the integrity of quantum communication channels. Management may need to redesign access control mechanisms to incorporate the principle of quantum superposition. Superposition enables quantum computers to solve mathematical problems more quickly than classical computers. Furthermore, governance frameworks must establish clear boundaries between classical and quantum processing environments to maintain security and compliance.

Agentic AI

IBM defines AI as "a technology that enables computers and machines to simulate human learning, comprehension, problem solving, decision making, creativity and autonomy."[21] An AI Agent is a program designed to perform tasks autonomously. These agents operate independently when making decisions, allowing the system to divide and conquer complex workflows with minimal human oversight. The authors believe that Agentic AI holds immense promise. They leverage cloud resources to perform tasks, make decisions, and adapt to changing environments effectively and efficiently.[22]

Agentic AI identifies patterns and learns from those patterns to adapt workflows and refine strategies. Agents can make informed decisions based on the context of a given scenario, enabling them to mimic human reasoning. AI agents are transforming various industries by automating tasks and making informed decisions. The authors believe that the deployment of AI Agents in the cloud enhances their capabilities, making them more efficient and effective.

Statista projects the market revenue has the potential to amount to USD 47 billion by 2030.[23] AI Agents are employed in various industries such as healthcare, customer service, retail manufacturing, and cybersecurity. AI Agents are revolutionizing the healthcare industry by providing diagnostic support. They can analyze radiology images, evaluate patient history, and recommend treatment plans. This personalized and proactive approach significantly adds value to patient healthcare services. In addition, Bernard Marr, a Futurist in the fields of business and technology, advances the idea that,

> AI agents could transform talent management by automating and enhancing various Human Resource (HR) processes. From conducting initial candidate screenings and scheduling interviews to managing employee onboarding and ongoing training, these agents could streamline HR operations. They could also provide personalized career development advice to employees based on their skills, performance, and company needs.[24]

There are no requirements for AI Agents to be built or run on cloud platforms. However, the cloud is where most of the agent development and deployment is taking place.[25]

The authors believes that market hype has led many to overestimate the current readiness of AI systems to deliver complex, autonomous capabilities at scale. At the same time, businesses have underestimated the necessary investment in data infrastructure, talent, and long-term financial commitment required to make these systems work.[26] Organizations must advance their governance frameworks from static policies to incorporate dynamic and adaptive controls. These controls should oversee Agentic AI while leveraging its capabilities to enhance cyber resilience and deliver value at an unprecedented scale and speed.

Cloud Gaming

Cloud gaming uses the connectivity of the 5G wireless network to allow the user to stream multimedia content from a cloud server to mobile phone devices, game consoles, laptops, and tablets. Cloud-based gaming eliminates the requirement for users to buy hardware and upgrade content. A high-definition cloud game requires low latency, large bandwidth, and low response time. The authors believe that cloud gaming represents a transformational shift in how digital entertainment is delivered and consumed, democratizing access to high-quality gaming experiences without the traditional hardware barriers.

Microsoft Xbox, Nvidia GeForce Now, and Sony Play Station offer cloud gaming products. The market for gaming is massive and growing. Companies like these must address governance challenges like data sovereignty, bandwidth provisioning, and latency to ensure a quality user experience. Statista projects the worldwide cloud gaming market will generate revenues of USD 18 billion by 2027.[27]

IoT

IBM defines the Internet of Things (IoT) as "a network of physical devices, vehicles, appliances, and other physical objects that are embedded with sensors, software, and network connectivity, allowing them to collect and share data."[28] Self-driving cars, smart thermostats, smart watches, and pacemakers are example IoT devices. Statista projects the worldwide IoT market will generate revenues of USD 2.2 trillion in 2028 and there will be 32.1 billion IoT devices in place globally by 2033.[29,30] See the call out box for a further discussion on IoT devices.

With expanding cloud infrastructures to support IoT ecosystems, the authors believe that organizations encounter complexity in managing environments that span multiple cloud providers, on-premises systems, and edge platforms. Different operating systems, protocols, and management tools add to this complexity. Security teams must tackle a landscape where cloud services interact with numerous IoT devices, each with specific vulnerabilities and compliance needs. Governance frameworks must adapt to address this diversity. Management should establish policies for hybrid environments while maintaining flexibility for various cloud-enabled IoT technologies.

Big Data Storage Solution

Streaming movies and games, leveraging quantum computers, using IoT devices, and creating Generative AI content generates large amounts of data, which creates the need for more storage capacity. The authors think this is where the benefits of the cloud are realized. Statista projects that by 2028, worldwide, the digital universe will create 394 zettabytes of data.[31] For context, one zettabyte is the equivalent of storing 250 billion DVDs.[32]

The DNA Data Storage Alliance is addressing the growing demand for archival storage based on DNA as a data storage medium.[33] "DNA as a storage device is an approach for storing digital information in DNA molecules. It is analogous to storing data on a computer hard drive, but instead of using magnetic or electronic technology, data are stored using chemical technology in the form of DNA molecules."[34]

Large amounts of data will require organizations and their CSPs to mitigate data privacy and security risks. Gartner highlighted that data risks demand extensive governance for the IoT.

> The scale and pace of data generated by "things" introduces integrity challenges and obviates traditional approaches that data and analytics leaders have used for data quality assurance. The highly distributed nature of IoT architectures challenges expectations on data availability, requiring data and analytics leaders to accept that purely centralized approaches to governance controls will become less viable.[35]

Call to Action

Each of the chapters in this book is interconnected and centered in a cloud governance ecosystem, as depicted in Figure 1.1. The reader may approach each individual chapter as separate, stand-alone articles on specific topics related to the cloud, which can be read in any order. Each chapter ends with a summary of practical actions for improving cloud governance. To conclude this first chapter, the authors highlight key practical actions aimed at enhancing cloud governance, which serve as a foundation for implementing effective strategies discussed throughout the book.

1. Leverage the budget considerations to formulate cost estimates for the business case for leadership to invest in the cloud.
2. Conduct a digital skills gap analysis of the organization's current workforce and implement strategies to address staffing and competency gaps.
3. Strengthen digital literacy and fluency of the members of the Board of Directors to evaluate whether to recruit Board members with cloud and AI experience.

4. Evaluate the risk portfolio and risk register to proactively manage and mitigate cloud and AI risks.
5. Conduct audits and assessments of the organization's cloud security and cloud compliance programs.

Box 1.1: Edge computing enables IoT

Edge architecture represents a pattern for system design, whereas IoT refers to the technology used to implement that pattern. Edge makes it possible to send, receive, and analyze data from IoT devices. Instead of sending the data to a centralized cloud data center, computing at the Edge can help an organization locally process data in real-time because the computing occurs at or near the user or source of data. According to RedHat, one of the benefits of Edge includes,

> The ability to conduct on-site big data analytics and aggregation, which is what allows for near real-time decision making. Edge computing further reduces the risk of exposing sensitive data by keeping all of that computing power local, thereby allowing companies to enforce security practices or meet regulatory policies.[36]

The authors believe Edge computing and IoT are interdependent. Edge influences cloud development, and the cloud provides the necessary infrastructure. Cloud Service Providers will continue to dominate AI and processing aspects of Edge computing, regardless of their ownership of Edge devices, by optimizing compute locations based on requirements.

Implanted medical and wearable health devices are examples of IoT devices that are emerging cloud technologies within the healthcare industry. Wearable health technologies are "small electronic devices that, when placed on the body, can help measure temperature, blood pressure, blood oxygen, breathing rate, sound, GPS location, elevation, physical movement, changes in direction, and the electrical activity of the heart, muscles, brain, and skin."[37] Consumers who use cloud-connected medical devices and wear health technology devices are susceptible to cybersecurity attacks. Cyberattacks affecting medical devices may delay essential patient care, expose sensitive patient information, and disrupt healthcare provider operations.

The U.S. Government Accountability Office identified "intentional threats" to implantable medical devices. IoT medical devices that transfer unencrypted data using wireless cloud technology are at risk to,

– "Unauthorized access: a malicious person intercepting and altering signals sent wirelessly to the medical device
– Malware: a malicious software program designed to carry out annoying or harmful actions and often masquerading as or embedded in useful programs so that users are induced to activate it
– Denial-of-service attack: computer worms or viruses that overwhelm a device by excessive communication attempts, making the device unusable by either slowing or blocking functionality or draining the device's battery."[38]

Unauthorized access to data generated by wearable technologies can be obtained by malicious hackers due to unsecured default configurations and weak encryption of IoT devices. Organizations must implement robust cloud data governance policies that document how data collected at the Edge from IoT-connected devices is stored, secured, and analyzed.

Box 1.2: Cloud Governance Success Story

Five years ago, a medium-sized organization embarked on an ambitious cloud transformation journey. With aging legacy systems struggling to meet modern demands, leadership recognized the need for change but underestimated the complexity of the transition. Initially, leadership made the classic mistake of treating cloud adoption as primarily a technical challenge. Management quickly learned that technology was only one component.

Early migration attempts faced resistance from managers and employees who felt excluded from the decision-making process. Organizational change management needed to be a fundamental aspect of cloud transformation. Leadership realized that to succeed, they needed to build trust. The IT team underwent training in human-centered design and product management to better understand business needs.

At first, the IT function moved legacy systems to the cloud without proper optimization, resulting in unexpected cost overruns and performance issues. The organization recognized they needed a more holistic cloud governance approach. Leadership pivoted by creating a formal cloud strategy with clear objectives aligned to outcomes. Instead of mandating cloud adoption, management brought together stakeholders from across the organization to collaboratively develop solutions and share best practices.

The organization implemented a shared responsibility model for cloud governance, distributing accountability across business units and Cloud Service Providers. Management created an inventory of cloud activity to maintaining centralized oversight. They developed a FinOps practice focused on overall value delivery as well as cost control. This transparent reporting allowed teams to track usage against budgets and identify optimization opportunities.

Management strengthened risk management protocols through comprehensive security assessments for cloud workloads. The organization created a pre-approved services catalog to ensure compliance while giving teams flexibility in implementation. The Internal Audit function conducted audits to comply with security and legal requirements, with quarterly results reported to the Board of Directors.

Leadership investment in learning and development proved crucial. The organization created training pathways for staff to develop cloud skills. This addressed technical needs and helped overcome resistance to change.

Five years later, the organization has transformed. Instead of eight data centers, they now operate two, with 60 percent of workloads running in the cloud. Application deployment time has decreased from months to days, and the organization has realized a 35 percent reduction in total IT operating costs. Beyond financial metrics, the most significant return has been increased business agility. New technology capabilities are deployed rapidly to meet emerging needs, and the organization is exploring Generative AI to enhance operations.

Management created a cloud governance framework that balanced innovation with responsibility. The cloud transformed the systems and how the organization works.

Chapter 2
The Dark Side of the Cloud

We become what we behold.
We shape our tools, and thereafter our tools shape us.[39]
– Marshall McLuhan, Philosopher

Introduction

The cloud's promise of infinite scalability comes at a dual cost. The cloud creates an ever-expanding attack surface for cybercriminals, it leaves harmful carbon footprints and contributes to Earth's water scarcity. The cloud exposes organizations to a wide variety of cyber-attacks, including data breaches, ransomware, malware, and supply chain attacks. AI-enabled cloud capabilities have introduced new ways malicious actors exploit AI models and training data. AI-powered cyber-attacks have become increasingly sophisticated, enabling adversaries to launch more targeted and effective campaigns against cloud infrastructure and sensitive data stored in the cloud. This chapter explores examples of cloud related cyber-attacks reported in the media. It also discusses how the cloud negatively contributes to water scarcity, harmful carbon emissions, and significant electricity consumption.

Information Technology Systems and Cyber-Attacks

Information technology systems are subject to cyber-attacks, including data breaches. What is a *cyber-attack*? The National Institute of Standards and Technology (NIST) defines a *cyber-attack* as:

> An attack, via cyberspace, targeting an enterprise's use of cyberspace for the purpose of disrupting, disabling, destroying, or maliciously controlling a computing environment/infrastructure; or destroying the integrity of the data or stealing controlled information.[40]

What is a *data breach*? NIST defines a *breach* as:

> The loss of control, compromise, unauthorized disclosure, unauthorized acquisition, or any similar occurrence where: a person other than an authorized user accesses or potentially accesses personally identifiable information; or an authorized user accesses personally identifiable information for another than authorized purpose.[41]

According to IBM's Cost of a Data Breach Report for 2024, "The average cost of a data breach jumped to USD 4.88 million from USD 4.45 million in 2023, a 10% spike and the highest increase since the pandemic."[42] Now, cyber-attacks have become increasingly sophisticated because of AI. Cybercriminals are maliciously leveraging AI to deceive people, produce harmful outputs, and engage in fraudulent activities. AI-enabled cyber-attacks are difficult to detect.

The Dark Side of the Cloud: Cloud Failures Reported in the Media

Market intelligence reveals that cloud computing exposes organizations to cyber-attacks and data privacy breaches. This disruptive cloud paradigm raises concerns from corporate boards, managers, regulators, and assurance providers concerning cloud strategy, performance, risks, and controls. The reality of cybersecurity risks in a cloud paradigm is evidenced by the growing number of cloud cyber-attacks and cloud breaches revealed by the media. No organization is immune from becoming a victim of cyber-attack. To gain insights into cloud cyber-attacks, the tables below highlight three significant cloud cyber-attacks reported in the media. Table 2.1 presents a summary of the attack on Ticketmaster.

Table 2.1: Summary of the Cyber-Attack on Ticketmaster, as adapted from Security Information Watch.[43]

Company: Ticketmaster	Ticketmaster is a ticket sales company with global operations. Ticketmaster is a subsidiary of Live Nation, which is an events promoter and venue operator.
What was nature of the Cyber-Attack?	Malware-as-a-Service (MaaS) A tool that specializes in gathering and exfiltrating sensitive data. The tool typically pulls users passwords from browsers' 'saved passwords' and then sends the credentials back to a central infrastructure. Those credentials are then collated, bundled together, and sold to the highest bidder on the Dark Web.
How did it happen?	In May 2024, hackers stole login details from a cloud database hosted by Snowflake, which is Ticketmasters' third-party CSP.
What was the impact of the Cyber-Attack?	Hackers stole personal details of 560 million Ticketmaster customers and attempted to sell the information on the dark web for $500,000 USD.

A *Supply Chain cyber-attack* on the company SolarWinds was unique in its scope of attack. As opposed to only attacking a single company, hackers gained access to the networks, systems, and data of SolarWinds customers. Table 2.2 presents a summary of the attack on SolarWinds.

Table 2.2: Summary of the Cyber-Attack on Solar Winds, as adapted from TechTarget.[44]

Company: SolarWinds	SolarWinds is a provider of software solutions designed to help monitor and manage the performance of customer IT systems.
What was the nature of the Cyber-Attack?	Supply Chain Cyber-Attack According to Microsoft, a supply chain cyber-attack is "an emerging kind of threat that target software developers and suppliers. The goal is to access source codes, build processes, or update mechanisms by infecting legitimate apps to distribute malware. Attackers hunt for unsecure network protocols, unprotected server infrastructures, and unsafe coding practices. They break in, change source codes, and hide malware in build and update processes."[45]
How did it happen?	Customers of SolarWinds inadvertently installed the malware that was part of the routine software updates (e.g., software patches, new versions of the software). The malware was used to gain unauthorized access to systems to spy on organizations, including the United States Government.
What was the impact of the Cyber-Attack?	More than 18,000 customers installed the malware and were affected by the breach. In an October 2023 class action lawsuit, SolarWinds paid $26 million USD to shareholders because SolarWinds neglected its cyber security internal controls and misled the public.

The cyber-attack on the company Blackbaud was a *ransomware cyber-attack*. Some estimates suggest that several million individuals had their personal identifiable information stolen from the illegal and undetected access of Blackbaud's systems. Table 2.3 presents a summary of the cyber-attack on Blackbaud.

Table 2.3: Summary of the Cyber-Attack on Blackbaud, as adapted from BankInfoSecurity.[46]

Company: Blackbaud	Blackbaud provides financial and fundraising software, systems, and services to not-for-profit organizations.
What was nature of the Cyber-Attack?	Ransomware Cyber-Attack "Ransomware is a form of malware that uses encryption to render files, data and/or systems unusable. Malicious actors then demand ransom in exchange for realizing the hostage systems, files and data."[47]
How did it happen?	In 2020, hackers illegally accessed and removed a copy of a subset of data from Blackbaud's systems.
What was the impact of the Cyber-Attack?	Hackers demanded ransom in return for a guarantee that the hostage information would not be misused or disseminated and would be destroyed.

These media reports of breaches demonstrate the reality of cloud-related cyber-attacks. Your organization can also be victimized of a cloud cyber-attack if management does not implement a cloud security program with strong internal controls and effective governance mechanisms.

Are You Surprised by the Wave of Cloud Cyber-Attacks?

The *dark side of the cloud* should come as no surprise to informed boards of directors, management, cloud risk and security professionals. Cautionary warnings concerning cloud cyber-attack vulnerabilities have been advanced for over decade. However, cloud-related cyber-attacks continue. In 2024, IBM released a report titled, *Cost of a Data Breach Report 2024.*[48] The following is only a small sample of the notable findings reported by IBM.

- The largest cost savings revealed in the report shows that when organizations deploy AI across their security operations center organizations, they averaged USD $2.2 million less in breach costs compared to those with no AI use in prevention workflows. Further, organizations that deployed AI detected and contained an incident, on average, 98 days faster than organizations not using AI security technologies.
- Compared to other vectors, malicious insider attacks resulted in the highest costs, averaging USD $4.99 million. Among other expensive attack vectors were the compromise of business email, phishing, social engineering and sto-

len credentials. Generative AI may be playing a role in creating some of these phishing attacks.
– The average cost of a data breach jumped to USD 4.88 million from USD 4.45 million in 2023, a 10% spike and the highest increase since the pandemic.

If there is a lesson to be learned from the onslaught of cybersecurity attacks that have occurred, it is that despite best efforts to guard against attacks, no organization is immune from becoming a victim of cyber-attack.

The Dark Side of the Cloud: Negative Effects on the Environment

Data centers require massive amounts of water and electricity to cool and operate the systems. GenAI and quantum computing will place heavy demands on cloud data centers. Goldman Sachs Research estimates that by 2030, global data center power demand will grow by 165% as compared to 2023[49]

The deployment and use of the AI-enabled cloud negatively contributes to water scarcity, harmful carbon emissions, and significant electricity consumption. For example, in 2023 Google's data centers and offices consumed more than 6.1 billion gallons of water.[50] In another example, researchers at University of California, Riverside estimated that ChatGPT gulps a 16-ounce water bottle (0.5 liters or 1 pint) each time a user asks it 5 to 50 prompts or questions. In terms of energy consumption, the same ChatGPT output is estimated to require 140 watt-hours of electricity.[51] For context, a keyword search uses 0.3 watt-hours of electricity, according to the International Energy Agency.[52] The development of AI training models and the use of GenAI is significantly and negatively contributing to the environmental effects across the globe. Most CSPs have initiatives in place to improve their water efficiency and reduce the use of potable drinking water to cool their data centers.

The landscape of power generation for data centers is shifting dramatically, with nuclear power emerging as a viable option for meeting the surging electricity demands of AI and the cloud.[53] Recent developments indicate a revival of nuclear energy through three pathways: restarting previously closed plants (like Three Mile Island Unit 1 and Palisades), upgrading existing facilities, and developing new reactor projects. Immediate energy needs will be met by gas, solar, and storage solutions. However, nuclear energy is expected to significantly contribute after 2030, especially for data centers demanding up to 5 gigawatts of power.[54]

While the authors have limited expertise in energy policy, the authors consider nuclear power to be a potential solution to balance environmental concerns with the substantial energy demands of the digital revolution. While renewable energy remains preferable from a sustainability perspective, its scalability limitations make it insufficient for the exponential growth in power demands from AI workloads. Nuclear offers a carbon-minimal alternative that can deliver the consistent, high-capacity generation needed for cloud operations without the environmental damage of coal. CSPs encounter high costs and lengthy timelines for nuclear projects but can gain long-term strategic benefits. Cloud governance should support a diversified energy strategy that includes nuclear power and continued expansion of renewable energy capacity. Companies are also exploring space as an alternative location to Earth to house their cloud data centers.[55,56]

Standard setting organizations, such as the Greenhouse Gas Protocol (GGP), have advanced sustainability reporting frameworks. The frameworks guide organizations how to disclose the impact and outcomes of their water, carbon, and electricity sustainability practices, such as cloud usage. Organizations that engage CSPs should structure Service Level Agreements to include the reporting of CSP greenhouse gas emissions and other significant environmental related performance metrics for the duration of the cloud services contract. To increase compliance reporting requirements, in September 2023, the European Union (EU) issued an energy efficiency directive that includes reporting requirements about environmental impacts of the cloud. The EU energy directive requires data centers to collect and report key sustainability metrics including energy efficiency, renewable energy usage, waste heat reuse, cooling effectiveness, carbon impact, and freshwater consumption. The EU will assess data center efficiency while providing a foundation for transparent planning and decision-making.[57]

Call to Action

1. Implement a cloud security program with strong internal controls and effective governance mechanisms to prevent and detect cloud breaches.
2. Use Security Configuration Management to correct harmful cloud configuration errors.
3. Ensure that management changes the manufacturer's predefined default password setting for new cloud implementations.
4. Educate the Board of Directors about their fiduciary duties related to cloud security breaches.
5. Structure Service Level Agreements to include the reporting of CSP greenhouse gas emissions and other significant environmental related performance metrics for the duration of the cloud services contract.

Chapter 3
The Basics of Cloud Computing

As consumers, we have so much power to change the world
by just being careful in what we buy.[58]
– Emma Watson, English Actress and Activist

Introduction

The purpose of this chapter is to introduce the basics of the cloud, including the various service models and deployment models. This chapter explores selection criteria that organizations may use to procure cloud services. This chapter also discusses the need for the organization to create and continuously update a so-called *cloud inventory* for management to have visibility into cloud activities to execute an effective cloud strategy, manage cloud performance, and advance cloud governance mechanisms.

In addition, this chapter introduces the topic of Artificial Intelligence (AI). As organizations master the foundations of cloud computing, they must also understand how AI is revolutionizing cloud capabilities and cloud governance. The relationship between AI and cloud computing is deeply symbiotic, with AI technologies serving as core components of cloud architectures while cloud platforms provide the essential foundation for AI deployment.

Defining Cloud Computing

Table 3.1 presents definitions of cloud computing from two government agencies.

Table 3.1: Definitions of Cloud Computing – Selected Examples.

Source	Definition of Cloud Computing
National Institute of Standards and Technology (NIST)[59]	NIST defines cloud computing as a means for enabling on-demand access to shared pools of configurable computing resources (e.g., networks, servers, storage applications, services) that can be rapidly provisioned and released.
European Network and Information Security Agency (ENISA)[60]	ENISA defines cloud computing as an on-demand service model for IT provision, often based on virtualization and distributed computing technologies.

For purposes of this book, the organization is the cloud customer. According to NIST, "a cloud consumer represents a person or organization that maintains a business relationship with and uses the service from a cloud provider."[61]

Defining Artificial Intelligence

Cloud computing and AI have formed a powerful symbiotic relationship in modern technology infrastructure. Table 3.2 lists four AI technologies.

Table 3.2: Artificial Intelligence Technologies. Source: IBM.[62]

AI Technology	Description
Artificial Intelligence	Enables computers and machines to simulate human learning, comprehension, problem solving, decision making, creativity and autonomy.
Machine Learning	Creates models by training an algorithm to make predictions or decisions based on data.
Deep Learning	A subset of machine learning that uses multilayered neural networks, called deep neural networks, that more closely simulate the complex decision-making power of the human brain.
Generative AI	Deep learning models that can create complex original content in response to a user's prompt or request.

Figure 3.1 illustrates the symbiotic relationship between the cloud and categories of AI.

The cloud provides massive computational resources, scalable storage, and specialized hardware that are needed to train and deploy AI models effectively. The cloud enables organizations to implement AI solutions without extensive capital investment because AI often require bursts of intensive computation. Cloud vendors offer pre-built AI services that provide organizations machine learning capabilities into their applications without employees needing deep expertise in AI development. The integration of the AI-enabled cloud manifests in practical applications such as automation, advanced analytics, and enhanced security measures. The cloud can help power emerging technologies like Generative AI and the Internet of Things. This intersection of cloud and AI technologies has accelerated innovation while raising important governance considerations and risks related to data privacy, bias, safety, and ethics.

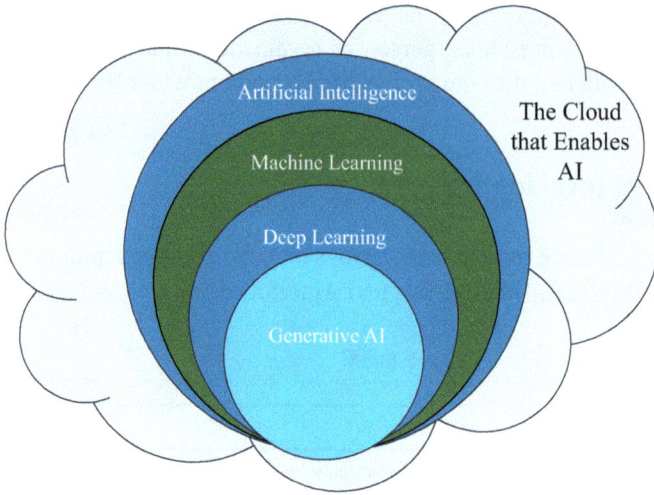

Figure 3.1: The Cloud Enabled-AI, Source: Authors.

Cloud Service Models

Cloud service models represent Cloud Service Provider (CSP) offerings to deliver cloud services to organizations. The CSP is the "person, organization, or entity responsible for making a service available."[63]

The organization's cloud strategy would determine which cloud service model management selects. Table 3.3 presents the three major cloud service models.

Table 3.3: Three Major Cloud Service Models. Source: NIST.[64]

Cloud Service Model	Description
Infrastructure as a Service (IaaS)	The CSP hosts, delivers, and manages the basic computing infrastructure of servers, software, storage, and network equipment. Organizations only pay for what they use.
Software as a Service (SaaS)	The CSP delivers and manages the infrastructure, operating system, and programming tools and services, which the customer can use to create applications.
Platform as a Service (PaaS)	The CSP delivers and manages one or more applications and all the resources (e.g., operating system and programming tools) and underlying infrastructure, which the customer can use on demand.

An emerging cloud service model is Quantum as a Service (QaaS). CSPs are offering this service for organizations to access quantum computing time without a significant capital investment to acquire a quantum computer.

The cloud provides organizations with the opportunity to outsource some, or all of their technology needs to a CSP. McKinsey offers these examples of how organizations are benefitting from the cloud: Example cloud services are:

- a retailer enhancing fulfillment, using AI to optimize inventory across channels and to provide a seamless customer experience
- a healthcare organization implementing remote heath monitoring to conduct virtual trials and improve adherence
- a high-tech company using chatbots to provide premier-level support combining phone, email, and chat
- an oil and gas company employing automated forecasting for supply-and-demand modeling and reducing the need for manual analysis
- a financial-services organization implementing customer call optimization using real-time voice recognition algorithms to direct distressed customers to experienced representatives for retention offers
- a financial-services provider moving applications in customer-facing business domains to the public cloud to penetrate promising markets more quickly and at minimal cost
- a health insurance carrier accelerating the capture of billions of dollars in new revenues by moving systems to the cloud[65]

According to Oracle,

> The cloud is becoming the go-to way to embed AI into business applications. Providers are baking AI into their own offerings, such as SaaS applications enhanced by a variety of AI technologies and more recently with embedded LLM capabilities. Cloud providers also work with businesses that want to embed generative AI into their operations.[66]

Cloud Deployment Models

An important strategic decision concerning the use of cloud computing is the selection of a cloud deployment model. According to NIST, cloud deployment models describe how the cloud is operated and who has access to the cloud service resources.[67] Table 3.4 lists popular cloud deployment models.

Table 3.4: Cloud Computing Deployment Models, as adapted from NIST.[68]

Cloud Deployment Model	Description
Single and Multi-Public Cloud	– Available to the public – Owned and operated by a CSP – Multi cloud means multiple public clouds
Single and Multi-Private Cloud	– Established for one organization; may involve multiple customers within that organization – Maybe on or off premises – Protected by powerful firewalls
Community Cloud	– Available to the public – Shared by several organizations and supports a specific community that has shared requirements – May be managed by the organization or a third party – May exist on or off premises – Industry cloud is a type of community cloud. An industry cloud is "a bundle of cloud services, tools, and applications that focus on the most important use cases in a specific industry. The most common industry clouds are designed for the retail, healthcare, government, and finance sectors."[69]
Hybrid Cloud	– A composite of two or more of the three deployment models (private, community, or public) – Bound together by technology that enables data and application portability – Sovereign cloud is a type of hybrid cloud. A sovereign cloud "helps organizations comply with the laws of specific regions and countries. A sovereign cloud mainly protects customer and organizational data."[70]

Another cloud deployment model that is emerging in the cloud ecosystem called a microcloud. According to ITPro Today, a publishing company, "microclouds offer the convenience of conventional cloud computing platforms but without restricting customers to hosting workloads inside cloud data centers. With a microcloud, you can place your workloads wherever you want."[71] Microclouds are an edge computing solution. Micro-cloud is also a term used to refer to smaller CSPs that are beginning to compete with full service CSPs known as hyperscalers. Micro-cloud CSPs offer several advantages over their larger [CSP] counterparts:

– Cost-Effectiveness: They often offer lower prices, especially for specialized services.
– Flexibility and Customization: They are more willing to tailor their offerings to meet the specific needs of their customers.

- Personalized Service: They provide a more hands-on approach, with dedicated account managers and technical support.
- Data Sovereignty and Security: They may offer more control over data storage and compliance with local regulations.[72]

Cloud Vendors and Criteria for Selection

The cloud ecosystem is comprised of a range of vendors providing distinct cloud services. Table 3.5 lists examples of cloud vendor roles and services.

Table 3.5: Categories of Cloud Vendors. Source: Authors.

Cloud Vendor Type	Cloud Roles and Services
Full-Service CSPs, including Hyperscalers	Market estimates suggest that over 500 vendors operate in some capacity as full-service CSPs offering public, private, and hybrid cloud services. Hyperscalers are CSPs that have a large share of the cloud market. – Hyperscalers are portrayed in the market as industry leaders because of their unique market share, which in turn enables them to offer services that improve scalability, interoperability, and compliance capabilities with evolving regulatory requirements. – Hyperscalers include Amazon, Microsoft, Google, Oracle, IBM, Apple, and Salesforce.
Managed Service Providers (MSP)	MSPs help organizations manage cloud services, including managing CSPs. MSP vendors provide organizations with continuous, regular management, maintenance, and support. Examples of MSP-related services include: – Hardware-as-a-Service (a recurring fee to access and use servers, storage, networking equipment, desktops, or other devices) – Network monitoring – System management – Human resources – Assessing service level compliance by CSP – Data backup and disaster recovery (storage only) – Email server hosting – Patch management – Software installations

Table 3.5 (continued)

Cloud Vendor Type	Cloud Roles and Services
Managed Security Service Providers (MSSP)	According to Gartner, an MSSP "provides outsourced monitoring and management of security devices and systems. Common services include managed firewall, intrusion detection, and vulnerability scanning."[73]
AI Service Providers (AISP)	According to the Cloud Security Alliance, an AISP is "an entity that provides AI services on demand to help users build AI applications. These entities could be CSPs such as Amazon, Microsoft, and Google, as well as other specialized providers."[74]

Several criteria will inform management's decision concerning which cloud vendor(s) to select to provide services. Table 3.6 list examples of important selection criterion.

Table 3.6: Descriptions of Vendor Selection Criteria. Source: Cloud Industry Forum.[75]

Cloud Industry Forum's Vendor Selection Criteria	Cloud Governance Implications
Certifications & Standards	CSP provides evidence to adhere to industry best practices, and compliance with standards and frameworks.
Technologies & Service Roadmap	Quality and availability of CSP technology services and deployment models align with the organization's cloud strategy. CSP provides a comprehensive cloud service roadmap. A service roadmap answers "three essential questions: Where are we now? Where do we want to go? and How can we get there?"
Data Security, Data Governance, and Business Policies	Poorly designed policies practices can lead to poor fiscal performance, compliance, regulatory fines and penalties, and destruction of reputation and stakeholder trust. Management should understand the proposed location and transfer process of data across jurisdictions, regions, states, and countries. For example, to reduce the risk of a cloud breach, management and the CSP must have safeguards in place to protect personally identifiable information.

Table 3.6 (continued)

Cloud Industry Forum's Vendor Selection Criteria	Cloud Governance Implications
Service Dependencies & Partnerships	CSP relationships extend responsibilities outside of the protective boundaries of the organization. CSP relationships are further exacerbated when the primary CSP vendor outsources an organization's cloud activities to other vendors, creating fourth- and fifth-party vendor risks.
Contracts, Commercials & SLAs	The organization – not the CSP – has the primary responsibility and accountability for the proper operation, performance, and governance of the cloud. Management must understand the scope of services and responsibilities that vary based upon the CSP. To efficiently manage cloud performance, an SLA should specify terms about data rights, data usage, and legal protections.
Reliability & Performance	CSP products and services should be reliable. However, downtime is inevitable. Management should ensure performance monitoring and reporting tools are available to manage service disruptions. Management should understand the frequency and impact of failures on its users. For example, the reliability performance level could be that the cloud application is available 99.99 percent of the time during business hours and 99 percent of the time on nights and weekends. A cloud *service outage* is an unexpected period of time during which cloud services are unavailable to the customer. If a CSP experiences an outage, then the organization can lose revenue and suffer damage to its reputation. For example, on October 4, 2021, Facebook and Instagram were unavailable for six hours. Facebook lost $60 million USD during that downtime.[76]
Business Health & Company Profile	Management often places substantial reliance on CSPs, including meeting cloud strategy, cloud governance, cloud operations, and cloud performance. Accordingly, organizations should perform due diligence to understand whether a CSP is a sustainable business that will continue to exist in the future.
Migration Support, Vendor Lock-In & Exit Planning	Vendor lock-in occurs when an organization using a cloud product or service cannot easily transition to a competitor CSP. For example, management should understand the CSP data ownership and retrieval rights upon term end.

AI is exacerbating the risk of cloud vendor lock-in. Organizations are using AI that may necessitate moving data from one cloud environment to another. Management would need to decide whether to use only the AI platforms that their CSP offers or spend resources to migrate to another AI service offered by another CSP. Leveraging a multi-cloud strategy provides management with an opportunity to spread AI workloads across CSPs.

Cloud Sprawl

After carefully evaluating and selecting a cloud vendor, organizations must remain vigilant about managing their cloud environment. Even with the right provider in place, the organization may encounter a phenomenon called *cloud sprawl*. According to TechTarget, "Cloud sprawl is the uncontrolled proliferation of an organization's cloud instances, services, or providers. Cloud sprawl typically occurs when an organization lacks visibility into or control over its cloud computing resources."[77]

Organizations experiencing cloud sprawl often face cloud complexity that can lead to failures. Cloud complexity is influenced by factors such as workloads, databases, storage systems, security models, management platforms, and governance models. For instance, an organization develops and migrates cloud applications in short, isolated phases. Subsequently, independent management efforts deploy cloud platforms without coordination or consideration for storage, security, and governance, leading to cloud complexity.[78] By implementing the robust cloud governance mechanisms described in this book, organizations can prevent cloud sprawl and achieve the transformational benefits of the cloud: optimal performance, innovation, increased productivity, cost savings, and much more.

Where Is My Cloud? The Need for a Cloud Inventory

Cloud sprawl creates a need for management to have visibility into and control over its cloud computing resources. A cloud inventory can play a crucial role. A cloud inventory is an inventory of the:
- Hardware
- Software licenses
- Data
- Locations (jurisdictions, regions, countries, states) of cloud servers
- Access rights
- Prioritization of critical outage points

–   Service type
–   CSPs

A cloud inventory can provide management with valuable and timely visibility into the nature, scope, and locations of all cloud activities. Importantly, an incomplete or out-of-date inventory can be equally, if not riskier than the lack of a complete, accurate and up-to-date cloud inventory. A comprehensive and real-time cloud inventory is a key element of cloud governance.

Creating a cloud inventory is a complex task and will be based on the unique characteristics of the organization and the unique nature and scope of cloud deployment. Management should ask these questions that need to be addressed concerning cloud deployment:

–   How many CSPs is the organization contracted to do business with?
–   Are service level agreements in place with all CSPs?
–   Do the primary CSP vendors outsource cloud activities to subcontractors?
–   How many cloud software licenses do we have?
–   Where is the backup server? Is the backup accessed via satellite or underwater cable?
–   What countries are the CSP servers located in that house our data?
–   Which global jurisdictions are we subject to? Are other jurisdictions accessing our data and surveilling our activities?

The call out box at the end of the chapter suggests who could be responsible for managing the cloud inventory. To create a cloud inventory, management can use a range of cloud tools and leverage CSP capabilities such as deploying an asset discovery tool, implementing a Cloud Access Security Broker, surveying the organization, and flagging suspicious IT-related purchases. To reduce manual processes, management can also leverage AI products to automate the creation of a cloud inventory. AI products can identify and categorize cloud activities to enhance the accuracy and completeness of a cloud inventory.

A cloud inventory can provide an organization with valuable and timely visibility into the nature, scope, and locations of all cloud activities. A lack of transparency creates substantial risks to cloud strategy, performance, security, compliance, and governance. It is essential to cloud governance for management to have access to real-time, accurate information about the extent by which the organization is deploying and using the cloud.

Call to Action

1. Perform due diligence and use tested selection criteria to evaluate potential CSPs.
2. To prevent vendor lock-in, gain an understanding of the CSP data ownership and retrieval rights upon term end.
3. Analyze existing service level agreements and determine whether gaps exist.
4. Create a cloud inventory.
5. Examine what countries are the CSP servers are located that house data.

Box 3.1: Who Is Responsible for Managing a Cloud Inventory

Who is responsible for creating and managing a cloud inventory? The organization has options for which functional unit should be responsible for creating and managing a cloud inventory:

– Chief Information Security Officer
– Chief Operating Officer
– Third-party Managed Service Provider or CSP
– Cloud Center of Excellence (CCOE)

A CCOE is "a is a multidisciplinary team of experts within an organization. The team develops and leads a strategy to support successful, uniform cloud adoption. It also helps business units implement cloud technologies that are secure, efficient and cost-effective."[79] In this capacity, the CCOE, or other designated functional unit, would play a crucial role in integrating and communicating with governance stakeholders, including the board of directors, compliance, security, risk management, CSPs, and assurance providers.

Lastly, the organization's legal department would also play a role because the legal department should maintain the records of contracts and service level agreements with all CSPs. The contracts and agreements are a valuable source of information for management to create the cloud inventory.

Part II: **A Look at the Context of Cloud Computing and AI**

Chapter 4
Cloud Strategy and Performance

> Greatness is not where we stand, but in what direction we are moving.[80]
> – Oliver Wendell Holmes, Jurist and Legal Scholar

Introduction

Organizations are striving to strategically optimize the spectrum of beneficial outcomes from cloud computing. At the same time, organizations need to manage the disruption and transformation created by the cloud. Further, AI technologies are transforming cloud by enabling more intelligent, adaptive, and automated cloud infrastructure and services. As organizations integrate AI capabilities into their cloud environments, management must create a cloud strategy that balances innovation, performance, and governance to achieve strategic outcomes. According to Bernard Marr, a futurist in the fields of business and technology,

> AI isn't just another service running in the cloud – it's the intelligent force optimizing every aspect of cloud operations. For businesses ready to embrace this paradigm shift, the rewards will be extraordinary: unprecedented efficiency, dramatic cost reductions, and performance levels that were once thought impossible.[81]

An Evolving Cloud Strategy

Organizations design business strategies at a range of levels. At a basic level, strategy consists of a vision (e.g., increase profitability); goals and objectives (e.g., reduce IT costs); desired outcomes (e.g., reduce IT costs by 20%); organizational performance (i.e., increase productivity) and performance management (e.g., response time).

Some organizations adopt a cloud-*first* strategy that emphasizes selecting the cloud as the first priority above all other options when considering replacements for legacy in-house IT applications. However, according to Gartner, more than 60% of organizations adopt a cloud-*smart* strategy that focuses on an approach that is customized to the unique characteristics of the organization.[82] The Cloud Security Alliance (CSA) outlined that,

> a cloud smart approach can lead organizations to a place where their costs are predictable and their workloads are optimized. This gives them a competitive edge to execute a sustainable digital transformation strategy that is aligned with the customer's needs and organizational goals.[83]

A cloud-smart strategy may include questions such as, *Which infrastructure is best suited from migration to the cloud?; Which services?; Which applications?* The call out box at the end of this chapter provides advice to management about legacy systems and cloud migration options.

Developing an Organization-Wide Cloud Strategic Plan

According to the Gartner, "a *cloud strategy* is a concise point of view on the role of cloud within the organization. It is a living document, designed to bridge between a high-level corporate strategy and a cloud implementation/adoption/migration plan."[84] A cloud strategy is deigned in a manner similar to any other organizational strategy. For instance, a cloud strategy would include a vision as to how cloud computing will be deployed within the organization. This vison would include:
– Measurable expected outcomes linked to strategic objectives
– A roadmap for organizational performance to migrate from legacy technology to cloud-based technology, applications, products, and services
– A plan to maintain the equilibrium between the cloud and advanced technologies (e.g., artificial intelligence)

A range of stakeholders may collaborate to create a cloud strategic plan and a cloud migration plan. Such stakeholders may be exclusively internal to the organization or consist of a combination of internal and external stakeholders. For instance, the COO (chief operating officer), the CIO (the chief information officer), the CTO (chief technology officer), and the CFO (chief financial officer). This team may be supported by the legal function, the risk management function, and the internal audit function. Third-party vendors may also contribute to the cloud strategy.

A cloud strategic plan conveys how, why, and when an organization will invest in, introduce, deploy, or escalate existing or new cloud initiatives to achieve a targeted set of beneficial outcomes. Gartner created a framework for developing a cloud strategic planning document consisting of ten major components. Table 4.1 presents these components.

The content of a cloud strategic plan will vary based on the unique attributes of the organization and the nature and scope of the cloud initiative. For example, size, industry sector, and the level of organizational capabilities. The call out box at the end of this chapter describes a Capability Maturity Model advanced by Carnegie Mellon University. Such models can help management identify capability needs (e.g., a cloud-enabled workforce) that will inform cloud strategic goals and objectives.

Table 4.1: Framework for Developing a Cloud Strategic Plan, as adapted from Gartner.[85]

Major Components of a Cloud Strategy	Guidance
1) Executive Summary	Summarize how the plan demonstrates business value.
2) Cloud Baseline: Terms of Reference	Identify all terms and associated definitions that appear within the cloud strategy to ensure all stakeholders understand the definitions.
3) Business Baseline: Strategic objectives mapped to expected outcomes and risks	Present why the organization is migrating to the cloud. – Present what the business is trying to accomplish, and whether it aligns with existing data center/business strategies. – Map the strategic business goals to the potential benefits of the cloud and to associated potential risks.
4) Service Strategy	Define overall service strategy for meeting the organization's technology requirements. – Decisions on if and when to use a CSP versus build or maintain capabilities on-premises or elsewhere (public versus private cloud). – Identify benefits and challenges with multi cloud / hybrid / public /private alternatives.
5) Financial Considerations	Evaluate and understand the financial impact of migrating from an in-house technology model to a model using CSP pay-as-you-go and / or subscription models.
6) Principles	Explicitly state key principles, such as the following: – Cloud First, Cloud Smart or other cloud strategy. – Key vendor-oriented considerations (skills, cost, etc.). – Leveraging a multi-cloud model and best of breed.
7) Current State Assessment	Inventory and understand the current state of the organization's technology / workloads, including ownership, dependencies and security requirements for the most critical / most expensive.

Table 4.1 (continued)

Major Components of a Cloud Strategy	Guidance
8) Cloud Security	Security is a shared responsibility (e.g., organization and CSP). Identifying roles and responsibilities in detail is critical. Many of the cloud security controls are enabled by an array of configuration options unique to individual CSPs. – While many of the traditional IT security principles and practices apply equally to the cloud, the policies, governance, and assurance requirements may differ. – The security differences created by the cloud should be integrated into the cloud strategy.
9) Supporting Elements / Enablers	Strategy must be aligned with supporting enablers (e.g., staffing, data center, architecture, Cloud Center of Excellence.

10) Exit Strategy from CSP Contracts	Crucial to have a CSP exit strategy.
	– Some regulators (e.g., some EU and financial services regulators), mandate the creation of a documented exit strategy.
	– The exit strategy should focus on answering *what, why and how* questions, including consideration of the following.
	  – Data ownership
	  – Backup
	  – Getting back your data
	  – Portability

Impact of Not Having a Cloud Strategy

Cloud strategy is crucial to capitalizing on cloud opportunities, achieving desired outcomes, and managing risks. A lack of proper cloud computing planning can lead to significant challenges and inefficiencies. Table 4.2 lists twenty-five risks that could result if an organization does not have a cloud strategic plan.

The topics in each chapter of this book represent the individual and interconnected components of a cloud governance ecosystem. Management must create a cloud strategy that balances the components of the cloud governance ecosystem to achieve innovation, performance, and strategic outcomes.

Table 4.2: Top 25 List of the Impact of Not Having a Cloud Strategic Plan, Source: Authors.

Impact of Not Having a Cloud Strategy – Top 25 (random order)

1. Unbridled vendor activities with organization assets
2. Overreliance on one CSP vendor (concentration risk)
3. Haphazard controls over the extended enterprise
4. Lack of accountability for respective cloud-shared responsibilities
5. Lack of prioritized cloud initiatives
6. Bifurcated cloud leadership within the organization
7. Ungoverned workarounds and reengineering needs
8. AI/cloud washing and upselling/overselling by vendors
9. Caught in the reactive cycle of addressing immediate technical issues rather than leveraging cloud capabilities for competitive advantage and innovation.
10. Lack of a skilled AI/cloud-enabled workforce to execute the strategy
11. No change management to guide the successful adoption of the cloud
12. Increasingly complex data governance
13. Ineffective incident response and inability to investigate root causes of cloud breach
14. Lack of disaster recovery plans
15. Failure to address poor configuration settings resulting in increased cybersecurity risk
16. Unaware of scope, frequency of cyber-threats, and unsuccessful attacks and breaches
17. Intellectual property loss due to data leakage through GenAI
18. Unsanctioned shadow IT and a lack of a reliable, real-time cloud asset inventory
19. Understatement of cloud costs with little consideration for change management, training, cyber insurance, business interruption costs, crisis management costs, and ransomware attacks
20. Failure to monitor usage, significant cost overruns, and financial waste
21. Pressure to rapidly adopt the cloud before prepared to do so causing success to take longer than expected
22. Rapidly shifting regulatory requirements that differ across geographic jurisdictions and a misalignment with organization AI/cloud-related policies
23. Customer loyalty challenged by cloud breaches and service downtime
24. CSP security policies and priorities not aligned with organization policies
25. Convoluted and complicated SLA and CSP contracts

Cloud Strategy Enablers

As with all strategic plans, a range of factors *enable* effective execution of the cloud strategy. Table 4.3 presents four types of enablers.

Table 4.3: Enablers of Cloud Strategy – Selected Examples. Source: Authors.

Cloud Strategy Enablers	Overview
Cloud Center of Excellence (CCoE)	According to TechTarget, – "A CCoE is a multidisciplinary team of experts within an organization. – The team develops and leads a strategy to support successful, uniform cloud adoption. – It also helps business units implement cloud technologies that are secure, efficient and cost-effective."[86]
Cloud Migration Plan	– Integral to the cloud strategic plan, the cloud migration plan is a detailed plan for moving on-premises IT systems to the cloud. – It is a more tactical level plan (e.g., at the level of each individual application or data set).
Cloud Performance Management	– Provides visibility into the value proposition of cloud adoption. – Such a system is designed to align cloud strategic objectives with expected outcomes and key performance measures (KPIs). – Such KPIs would be monitored, reported and responded if cloud performance is not meeting expectations.
Flexible Cloud Strategy	– Avoid sticking to a fixed strategy in the face of substantial changes in the competitive and technology environment. – Leverage process improvements attained through maturity and adoption of best practices and the wisdom generated through the concepts of lessons learned and root cause analysis.

Cloud Performance Management and Key Performance Indicators (KPIs)

Management has a role in monitoring and measuring performance about the progress made to execute the cloud strategy. Performance management is integral to organizational strategy, success, and governance. A 2024 Cloud Computing Study conducted by Foundry stated that performance and reliability are challenges that have slowed or stalled cloud adoption at organizations.[87]

Cloud performance management, and associated KPIs, provide an early warning of the risks of failing to achieve the expected outcomes from the cloud. Cloud KPIs are designed to evaluate *actual* progress on performance results against *expected* strategic outcomes. Management can customize and develop cloud performance indicators to measure cloud *performance, reliability, availability, capacity, scalability,* and *cost.* Table 4.4 presents examples of cloud objectives and KPIs.

Table 4.4: Examples of Cloud Service Objectives and KPIs, as Adapted from Flexera's 2024 State of the Cloud Report.[88]

Cloud Service Objective	Examples of Cloud KPIs
Performance	– Response time for service – Completion time for tasks – Number of transactions or requests per specified unit of time
Reliability	– Measured as a percentage of time that the cloud service is working properly
Availability	– Service and system availability – Mean time between failure – Mean time to repair
Capacity	– Service bandwidth – Speed of processor – Storage capacity
Scalability	– Ability to support a defined or projected growth scenario – Yes or no metric or a metric that defines upper limit of scalability – Manage software licenses – Move on-premise software to SaaS – Migrate more workloads to the cloud – Progress on execution of the cloud strategy – Expanded use of containers – Increase use of public cloud
Cost	– Cost savings – Better financial reporting of cloud cost

Table 4.5 presents examples of performance and availability level service targets.

Inadequate cloud governance is another challenge to comprehensively managing cloud performance. For instance, the common problem of cloud misconfigurations is a major threat to cloud governance, contributing to cloud risk. Crowdstrike, a cybersecurity firm, defines misconfigurations as "the gaps, errors and vulnerabilities that occur when security settings are poorly chosen or neglected entirely."[89]

The organization should monitor cloud service level performance and hold vendors accountable for service failures. At designated intervals, management would use the performance data to develop, report, monitor, and respond to improve the cloud service objectives. Cloud Service Level Agreements (SLAs) should

Table 4.5: Examples of Reliability and Availability Service-Level Targets, Source: Authors.

Category	Service-Level Targets
Reliable Performance Levels	Outage: CSP will respond immediately and will attempt to resolve the issue in 2 h
	End-user Impacted: CSP will respond within 20 min and will attempt to resolve the issue within 12 h
	Potential for performance issue if not addressed: CSP will respond within 30 min and will attempt to resolve the issue within 24 h
Availability Performance Levels	99.99%; annual downtime is 50 min; 4 min per month
	99%; annual downtime is 3 days per year; 7 h per month
	95%; downtime is 18 days per year; 2 days per month

include remedies for when CSP performance problems emerge. The call out box at the end of this chapter presents key information about cloud SLAs.

Budget Considerations

The budget considerations to create and maintain a cloud strategy for a medium-sized organization ranges from USD $80,000 and USD $350,000. This amount can vary based on several factors including industry requirements and constraints, organization size and complexity, scope of cloud transformation, cloud maturity level, organizational culture and resistance, rate of desired cloud adoption, need for specialized expertise, and the timeline for implementation. The common budget allocations include:

- Cloud strategy development: USD $30,000–80,000 (higher in the first year)
- Cloud strategy leadership: USD $60,000–150,000
- Strategy execution oversight: USD $20,000–50,000
- Cloud architecture guidance: USD $25,000–70,000
- Strategic vendor management: USD $15,000–40,000
- Strategy review and updates: USD $10,000–30,000
- Advisory services/consultants: USD $20,000–80,000 (higher in the initial phase)

Management may adopt a phased approach, beginning with a substantial initial investment to develop the strategy and create a comprehensive roadmap. This should be followed by lower ongoing costs for updating the strategy. On a quarterly basis, management could revise the strategy to account for evolving business requirements, technological advancements, and competitive pressures. Additionally, on an annual basis, management can refresh the strategy to ensure alignment with overall business objectives.

Call to Action

1. Request that the CIO report to the Board of Directors about how the AI and cloud strategy align with the organization's business strategy.
2. Evaluate and decide which legacy applications can be migrated to the cloud, modernized, or remain on-premises.
3. Develop cloud performance indicators to measure cloud performance, reliability, availability, capacity, scalability, and cost.
4. Adopt financial governance protocols to manage cloud costs and measure the return on investment.
5. Leverage the Capability Maturity Model to evaluate the current level of maturity against benchmarks, establish a baseline, and track progress for improvement.

Box 4.1: Capability Maturity Model

A cloud computing strategy should address the organizational capabilities needed to adopt cloud technologies. To support the development of these capabilities, an organization should evaluate the current level of maturity against benchmarks and set prioritized goals for continuous improvement.

Carnegie Mellon University's Software Engineering Institute advanced the Capability Maturity Model (CMM) for organizations to improve and institutionalize their software process. Carnegie Mellon states that "higher degrees of institutionalization translate to more stable processes that are repeatable, produce consistent results, and over time are retained during times of stress."[90] Table 4.6 lists the levels of the Carnegie Mellon CMM and provides examples in context of the cloud.

Another resource for organizations to benchmark their maturity is the Open Alliance for Cloud Adoption, which maintains a cloud maturity model.[92]

Table 4.6: Levels of a Maturity Model, as Adapted from Carnegie Mellon University's Software Engineering Institute.

Capability Maturity Model Level[91]	Description	Cloud Examples
1. Initial	– Lack of organizational-wide capabilities – Inconsistent use – No clear stakeholder engagement – No documentation	– No cloud strategy – Fragments cloud use by business unit or by individual employee efforts – Allocates resources discretely (e.g., single workload or project) – No Service Level Agreements – Gaps in cloud skills exist
2. Repeatable	– Approach is not systematic	– Maintains weak cloud security controls – Lacks an understanding of the cloud shared responsibility model
3. Defined	– Standard process exists – Some familiarity amongst stakeholders	– No comprehensive cloud asset inventory exists
4. Managed	– Monitor and control process – Stakeholder buy-in – Evaluate performance	– Documents cloud strategy – Maintains a strong cloud security program – Documents and enforces SLAs – Conducts internal audits of the cloud – Upskills employees on the cloud – Obtains reasonable assurance that CSP complies with international regulations
5. Optimizing	– Continuous and routine monitoring	– Documents and uses cloud strategy to inform decisions – Establishes Cloud Center of Excellence – Continuously evaluates CSP performance using Cloud Key Performance Indicators – Maintains mature incident response capabilities to prevent, detect, and correct cloud breaches – Oversees and communicates financial impact of the cloud – Institutes strong cloud governance

Box 4.2: Financial Governance

The cloud disrupts organizational governance by altering how organizations manage and forecast costs, leading to inefficiencies and challenges. Traditional IT governance relies on predictable, capital-based budgets where resources are purchased upfront and depreciated over time. However, cloud computing shifts this model to an operational expense structure with often unpredictable, usage-based billing. Without proper governance frameworks, organizations struggle to track and control escalating costs caused by fluctuating consumption patterns.[93]

The lack of financial governance can result in cloud costs spiraling out of control. In an extreme example, Pinterest, the image-sharing and social media company, spent USD $190 million on cloud services with one vendor, USD $20 million more than it expected.[94] To mitigate such financial risks, organizations must have financial governance protocols in place to track and control expenditures.

Poor visibility into expenditures undermines cost management. Management should analyze and report cloud usage patterns to throttle capacity to effectively manage cost. Effective financial governance provides visibility into cloud spend and helps identify underutilized resources for management to make decisions to terminate certain cloud activities and make course corrections. Governance also encompasses financial forecasting and analysis. By evaluating cloud consumption trends, organizations can predict future costs and develop proactive expense management strategies. Table 4.7 presents Flexera's suggested activities to govern cloud cost.

Table 4.7: Financial Governance Measures, Source: 2024 Flexera State of the Cloud Report.[95]

Examples of Cloud Financial Governance Measures
– Govern IaaS/PaaS usage/cost
– Optimize SaaS usage/cost
– Govern software licenses in IaaS and PaaS
– Define cloud cost management policies
– Charge back cloud costs (to business units)
– Report and analyze cloud cost
– Own cloud budgets
– Optimize cloud spend
– Forecast cloud cost, post-migration

MSPs and CSPs offer a range of tools to help plan, track, and manage cloud costs. Tools can help organizations allocate costs to specific projects or functions. Example tools include billing reports and alerts, cost calculators, and detection capabilities for usage anomalies. Gartner recommends the use of the following cost metrics:
- Trending patterns daily, monthly, quarterly, and annually
- Actual versus planned spending
- Percentage of the overall spending
- Top spenders and least spenders, by business unit
- Estimated spending waste[96]

Box 4.3: Managing Cloud Performance

Analyzing and measuring the Return on Investment (ROI) of the cloud is also essential to managing cloud performance. VMware suggests the following considerations:

> Cloud ROI is impacted by initial outlay, the speed with which returns occur, and cost decreases that occur as a result of the investment. ROI has both tangible and intangible components – a complete ROI picture must include factors such as overall corporate value, customer goodwill, and brand value in the marketplace, to name a few.[97]

Remedies for When CSPs do not Meet Performance Levels

When CSP service level performance problems emerge, the organization and the CSP should work together to understand the root cause of the problem, the impact, and the action plan to correct the issue. If the CSP is unable to resolve the issue, then management should consider seeking remedies from the CSP. For example, a credit towards a portion of the monthly service fee. The organization should modify the SLA as necessary to address these issues should they arise again in the future.

Exit Strategy

In some cases, an organization dissatisfied with the performance of their CSP may decide to cancel their existing services with the CSP and transfer the services to a new CSP. This is often referred to as an *exit strategy*. It is important for an organization to document clear and specific exit strategy terms in the SLA *before* the organization migrates data and applications to the cloud. Management should build the estimated cost of the exit into the cloud migration business case.

Box 4.4: Legacy System Migration Decisions

When developing a comprehensive cloud computing strategy, organizations must make critical decisions about their existing legacy systems. Transitioning to cloud environments requires careful evaluation of which legacy applications can be migrated, modernized, or remain on-premises. Table 4.8 compares the benefits of on-premises versus cloud environments.

Table 4.8: Comparison of the Benefits of On-Premises Versus Cloud Environment, Source: Authors.

Objective	On-Premises	Cloud
Infrastructure Ownership	Organization owns and maintains all hardware	CSP owns and maintains infrastructure
Capital Expenditure	High upfront costs for hardware/software	Minimal upfront investment
Operational Expenditure	Lower recurring costs, higher maintenance	Higher recurring subscription costs
Cost Management	Difficult to attribute costs	Detailed reports of usage but risk of cost overruns and waste if not managed
Physical Security	Managed by the organization	Managed by the CSP

Table 4.8 (continued)

Objective	On-Premises	Cloud
Geographic Reach	Known physical locations managed by organization	Global infrastructure with risk of data residing across multiple jurisdictions
Responsibility for Security and Compliance	Organization has complete control of all systems and handles all updates and patches Shared responsibility with specific services for compliance	Shared responsibility model with the CSP
Disaster Recovery	Requires significant investment in redundant systems	Built-in redundancy options
Accessibility	Accessible in areas with limited or no internet connectivity	May experience service disruptions and downtime
Scalability	Limited by physical infrastructure and requires procurement of additional hardware	On-demand resources that can be added and removed quickly to meet business needs
Talent	Deep infrastructure expertise	AI and cloud-enabled workforce
Agility	Limited by IT function bandwidth and capabilities	Accelerated innovation enabled by CSP services to include GenAI and Quantum Computing
Environmental Impact	Less efficient individual data centers needing potable water and a lot of energy to cool and power	Economies of scale could equate to resource efficiency
Governance Model	Controlled at the centralized IT function	Distributed capability with centralized policies

Cloud solutions offer enhanced flexibility, whereas on-premises infrastructure ensures greater control and ownership. Many organizations benefit from integrating both on-premises systems with cloud services, thereby leveraging the advantages of each approach. A hybrid cloud model provides the flexibility and scalability inherent to public cloud, combined with the security and control characteristic of private infrastructure. This strategy also assists organizations in reducing their physical IT hardware requirements. McKinsey has found that,

> the value cloud generates from enabling businesses to innovate is worth more than five times what is possible by simply reducing IT costs. Cloud computing, among other technologies, can help companies go through the phases of a digital transformation faster and more efficiently. The benefits are faster time to market, simplified innovation and scalability, and reduced risk.

The cloud lets companies innovate quickly, providing customers with novel digital experiences. It also enables organizations to use bespoke, cutting-edge analytics not available on legacy platforms.[98]

Organizations should align their approach to legacy technology with broader business objectives, considering factors such as operational costs and organizational agility. A well-designed cloud migration roadmap acknowledges both the constraints imposed by legacy systems and the transformative opportunities that cloud adoption presents. Table 4.9 outlines the U.K. National Audit Office's advice on managing legacy systems and cloud migration options.

Table 4.9: Options for Legacy Technology in Cloud Migration, Source: UK National Audit Office.[99]

Decision	Description
Retain (do nothing)	Where the system is not cloud-compatible but is otherwise working well and there is no strong business case for the cost and disruption of moving to an alternative.
Retire	Where the system's functions are either no longer required or can be incorporated into other applications.
Repurchase ('shop and drop')	Decommissioning the existing application and replacing it with its equivalent cloud-based version. In effect it is a change in licensing arrangements alongside the work required to move the service into the cloud.
Rehost ('lift and shift')	Moving the application from on-premises to the cloud with no or only minimal modification to adapt to the new environment. It means that the application is unlikely to be able to take advantage of cloud-specific features but may be the only feasible option where organizations do not have the ability to make the necessary changes themselves. This may be the case for commercial off-the-shelf applications or customized applications built using proprietary technology that imposes constraints. This option is sometimes called 'moving without improving.'
Replatform ('lift and shape')	Modifying and optimizing the application for moving to the cloud, but not to the extent of significantly changing the core functions.
Refactor (rewrite)	This is the most complex option and involves a major overhaul of the application. It is very time-consuming and resource-intensive but offers the greatest opportunity for making extensive use of cloud capabilities.

Chapter 5
Cloud-Driven Change Management and Learning

> The greatest danger in times of turbulence is not the turbulence –
> it is to act with yesterday's logic.[100]
> – Peter Drucker, Inventor of Modern Management

Introduction

Large scale deployment of the cloud requires new skills and requires changes to existing organizational governance protocols. Effectively managing these and other cloud-related changes is crucial to achieving cloud strategy, performance, and governance objectives. This chapter discusses change management, learning, and development considerations associated with the large-scale deployment of the cloud.

Cloud-Driven Organizational Change

Large scale adoption of the cloud represents a large-scale *organizational change.* Organizational change spans a continuum, with incremental adaptive change at one end, and large-scale transformational change at the other end. Table 5.1 defines each of these endpoints.

Table 5.1: Definitions of Adaptive and Transformation Change, as Adapted from HBS Online.[101]

Change	Overview
Adaptive Change	Small, incremental adjustments that organizations make to adapt to daily, weekly, and monthly business challenges. Often related to fine-tuning existing processes, products, and company culture, and don't fundamentally change the organization as a whole.
Transformational Change	A dramatic and at times sudden (e.g., pandemic response) evolution of some basic structure of the business itself (e.g., AI strategy, culture, organization, physical structure, supply chain, or processes).

Smaller-scale adoption of cloud applications and services generally represent an adaptive change. Large scale deployment of the cloud represents a *transformational* organizational change. There are four components of how the cloud uniquely drives transformational change.

1. The Cloud Changes the On-Premises IT Function in an Organization

One major factor causing such a transformation of the in-house IT function is the use of CSPs. Cloud vendor adoption significantly reduces or eliminates the IT department's traditional infrastructure roles. IT organizations must rapidly shift their focus to mastering cloud technologies and integrating them with existing systems. See the call out box at the end of this chapter for additional insights on the role of the Chief Information Officer.

Another major factor causing the disruption of the in-house IT function is the democratization of IT, including cloud and AI technologies. When organizations grant employees true autonomy, management unlocks remarkable potential for innovation. By empowering employees to take ownership of digital transformation initiatives, explore creative solutions, and automate processes with applications like GenAI, organizations can tap into the full capabilities of their workforce. This shift from top-down control to democratization also creates an environment where the organization is at risk of violating cloud security laws, regulations, and policies. Management can proactively address these transformative impacts of the cloud on the in-house IT function by implementing the Calls to Action listed at the end of each chapter of this book.

2. The Cloud Disrupts Organizational Governance

Deploying the cloud at scale transforms organizational governance. A primary driver is the substantial increase in the reliance on a *shared responsibility model* for cloud governance. The following stakeholders are often involved in a cloud shared responsibility model.

– Employees – Democratized IT Organizational employees authorized to engage directly with CSPs to procure AI and cloud technologies.
– Employees – Shadow IT Activities Shadow cloud activities represent the unauthorized and unknown use of AI and cloud activities by front-line organizational employees outside of the purview of the centralized IT function and organizational governance functions.
– Third-Party Cloud Vendors include CSPs and MSPs.
– Organizational Governance Functions with IT and cloud-related roles such as the compliance function, internal audit, and the Board of Directors.

Transformation of the compliance function is an example of a cloud-driven change to an organizational governance function. According to Lucidchart,

With the cloud in use, your organization may have to set new internal policies for employees and should consider how changing compliance should be managed. If, for example, your organization is subject to PCI, GDPR, or HIPAA compliance, part of your change management would involve anticipating how these regulations impact your cloud transition and use.[102]

Management must transform organizational governance functions and protocols to properly integrate and respond to a cloud shared-responsibility model.

3. The Cloud Must be Managed

Another cloud-driven change is the creation of a new *cloud management* process. In-house IT functions, cloud shared responsibility models, and cloud governance protocols (e.g., compliance function) must transform to properly integrate and respond to a new cloud management process.

Red Hat defines cloud management as: "A combination of software, automation, policies, governance, and people that determine how cloud computing services are made available."[103] In the IT domain, cloud management is an element of an IT Service Management (ITSM) process. ITSM activities involve day-to-day, end-to-end delivery of IT operations and services such as software updates. Alternatives for deploying cloud management include the use of third-party cloud management platforms and the establishment of a Cloud Center of Excellence.

4. The Cloud Creates a Digital Skill Gap

A digital skill gap, including cloud and AI expertise, is a significant risk for organizations. A survey based on 1,215 respondents in global C-suite and board positions, conducted by North Carolina State University and Protiviti, reported on top organizational risks. Results indicated that the ninth top risk for year 2024 and the projected number four risk for year 2035 is the "adoption of AI and other emerging technologies requiring new skills in short supply."[104] Organizations must be ready for the type of transformation the world will experience with the use of Generative AI and Agentic AI.

The digital skill gap affects the organization's workforce and challenges organizational governance functions. Members of the board of directors also need an adequate level of AI and cloud-literacy to effectively exercise their cloud governance responsibilities.

Cloud-Driven Change Management

The deployment and operation of an effective *organizational change management* strategy and process is crucial to cloud governance. According to Lucidchart,

Effective change management smooths the transition to the cloud and gives organizations better insight throughout the process. Given the monumental changes associated with moving to the cloud, you need a change management strategy to manage risk and minimize wasted effort or cost.[105]

The American Society for Quality defines change management as,

The methods and manners in which a company describes and implements change within both its internal and external processes. Including, preparing, and supporting employees, establishing the necessary steps for change, and monitoring pre- and post-change activities to ensure success.[106]

While essential, organizational change management is inherently complex, time consuming, costly, and risky. According to Enterprisers Project, a community and online technology publication,

Executing a successful change management effort is one of the toughest challenges for an organization, regardless of how much money, brainpower, talent, and resources you may have at your disposal.[107]

A major part of the IT change management challenge is the risk of not fully and effectively achieving the outcomes expected from deploying technology. Leveraging well-established change management frameworks can contribute to effective IT change management.

Change Management Frameworks

Many frameworks exist for managing wide-scale transformational change in organizations. Management must customize change management frameworks to accommodate the unique impact of cloud-driven organizational change. Four popular frameworks were developed by John Kotter, Information Technology Infrastructure Library, American Society for Quality, and Prosci. Each change management model:

- Highlights the critical role of leadership in driving change
- Emphasizes the need for consistent measurement and monitoring
- Recognizes the importance of training and skill development
- Incorporates resistance management strategies
- Emphasizes the importance of celebrating successes
- Includes methods for gathering and acting on two-way communication feedback
- Stresses the need for continuous and clear communication at every stage

In addition to addressing cloud-driven organizational change, management must also secure employee support to effectively implement AI. This requires involving employees on planning, communicating the vision for innovation objectives, and proactively addressing automation concerns. Organizations should establish clear career progression paths and provide employees with AI training opportunities. These steps help transform employee uncertainty into enthusiasm for driving AI adoption and innovation.

Moving From the Digital Skill Gap Toward a Cloud Enabled Workforce

Organizations and CSPs are concerned about attracting and retaining talent in the cloud domain. Some organizations are leaning in to contribute to filling this gap. For instance, in 2020, Amazon announced their commitment to train 29 million people in cloud computing by 2025. Earlier than expected, by July 2024, Amazon had trained more than 31 million people worldwide. Between November 2021 and August 2023, Amazon opened three AWS Skills Centers located in the United States and South Africa. These centers provide free cloud computing training to the public. In 2024, Amazon also provided free training in AI to 2 million people.

This massive training initiative reflects the growing importance of understanding how the workforce can adopt the AI-enabled cloud across different roles and industries. *What is a cloud workforce*? With respect to roles, a cloud workforce consists of several cohorts of stakeholders that directly or tangentially play a role in the cloud. For instance, the in-house IT function; frontline business employees; the board of directors; and CSPs.

What is a cloud-enabled workforce? A cloud-enabled workforce is equipped with the skills necessary to drive cloud success. *Why is a cloud-enabled workforce crucial to cloud success?* According to Deloitte, the people-side of the cloud is essential to achieving strategic outcomes expected from the cloud.

> The challenge, however, is what we call the "cloud adoption plateau" – a stall in cloud adoption and true organizational transformation – that limits what organizations are able to achieve with cloud. Organizations may experience this plateau when they move too quickly to migrate work (applications and processes) to the cloud without developing the right operating model, skills, leadership support, and new ways of working.

> In essence, they haven't re-architected work for the cloud. These shortfalls have a business cost and an innovation cost – this is where HR leaders have an important opportunity to work with IT and business leaders to help overcome them. That means creating a cloud-enabled organizational structure and workforce that is ready to support the organization's cloud transformation strategy, close innovation gaps, and enable sustained cloud ROI.[108]

How does an organization achieve a cloud-enabled workforce? Through a change management strategy. Transforming into a cloud-enabled workforce is a component of *the people-side* of change management. Cloud adoption demands both acquiring new technical skills and fostering a cultural shift in how teams approach operations and strategy. The Object Management Group's Cloud Working Group presents a perspective on a cloud-enabled workforce.

> Cloud computing and related technologies like blockchain, data science and artificial intelligence is transforming the nature of IT resulting in skill shortages in some domain areas and staffing surpluses in other traditional IT domains. As businesses consolidate data centers and relocate or virtualize workloads on-premises or via external cloud service providers, the needs for certain data center positions (e.g., facility monitoring/management, server setup and configuration, etc.) sharply diminish.
>
> A new set of domain skills around process automation, architecture, resource optimization and cost management are required to drive cloud-based initiatives. A solid understanding of infrastructure, middleware, and application concepts in the context of the enterprise business model is critical.[109]

Organizations facing digital skill gaps have a continuum of options available to work towards a cloud-enabled workforce. Five examples are presented in Table 5.2.

Table 5.2: Options for Addressing Gaps in Cloud Skill – Selected Examples, Source: Authors.

Option	Overview
Permanent Hires	Hire employees with the requisite cloud and AI skills to create a cadre of employees with the skills needed to address the full spectrum of cloud competencies (e.g., cloud strategy, deployment, scaling operations, technology, governance, etc.). A major challenge of this option is the high demand for digital talent globally and limited supply. This option also needs substantial time to scale.
Temporary Rotations	Temporary role rotations for full time employees through technology functional roles to shadow specialist and gain hands-on experience.
Temporary Staffing	Hiring temporary employees with the requisite AI and cloud-skills on a contract basis contributes to addressing immediate-term and short-term cloud-resource needs. The benefits of this outsourcing-type model are the ability to secure resources with the precise level of skills needed, just-in-time. A major challenge of this approach however is that it is not a permanent solution to embedding AI and cloud skills into the organization for the long-term.

Table 5.2 (continued)

Option	Overview
Reliance on Vendors (e.g., MSPs and CSPs)	Organizations are increasingly relying on vendors to supplement shortages in skills and resources. Benefits include real-time access to skills and resources. The major challenge of this option is cost.
Learning & Development (L&D)	Designing learning interventions to develop cloud skills for existing employees. A major benefit of this option is employees with critical institutional knowledge add requisite AI and cloud skills to their competencies. A major challenge is ensuring L&D interventions can be practically applied to the workplace.

Cloud-Related Learning & Development Considerations

L&D interventions are integral to a cloud-enabled workforce and effective change management strategies. The Academy to Innovate HR defines organizational L&D as,

> A systematic process to enhance an employee's skills, knowledge, and competency, resulting in better performance in a work setting. Specifically, learning is concerned with the acquisition of knowledge, skills, and attitudes. Development is the deepening of knowledge in line with one's development goals.[110]

The goal of learning and development is to change employee behavior, share knowledge and insights that enable them to do their work, and cultivate attitudes that help employees perform.

L&D Frameworks

The McKinsey ACADEMIES Framework can assist management with the development and customization an organization's cloud-related L&D strategy. Tables 5.3 outlines the dimensions of the popular framework.

Another popular L&D framework is ADDIE. Such learning frameworks may be used to develop a customized cloud learning strategy that includes defining learner needs, designing, developing, and delivering cloud training.

Table 5.3: Overview of the ACADEMIES Framework, as Adapted from McKinsey.[111]

#	Step	Overview
	**The McKinsey ACADEMIES Framework: Dimensions of a Strong L&D Function**	
1.	**A**lignment with business strategy	The learning strategy supports professional development and builds capabilities across the company, on time, and cost-effectively. In addition, the learning strategy can enhance the company culture and encourage employees to live the company's values.
2.	**C**o-ownership between business units and HR	L&D functions establish a governance structure in which leadership from both groups share responsibility for defining, prioritizing, designing, and securing funds for capability-building program. Executives help embed the learning function and all L&D initiatives in the organizational culture. The involvement of senior leadership enables full commitment to the L&D function's longer-term vision.
3.	**A**ssessment of capability gaps and estimated value	Take a deliberate, systematic approach to capability assessment, leveraging a comprehensive competency or capability model. After identifying essential capabilities for functions or job descriptions, assess how employees' rate in each of these areas. L&D interventions should seek to close these capability gaps.
4.	**D**esign of learning journeys	Continuous learning opportunities that take place over a period of time and include L&D interventions such as fieldwork, pre- and post-classroom digital learning, social learning, on-the-job coaching and mentoring, and short workshops. The main objectives are to help people develop the required new competencies in the most effective and efficient way and to support the transfer of learning to the job.
5.	**E**xecution and scale-up	Successful execution of L&D initiatives on time and on budget is critical to sustaining support from business leaders. Many new L&D initiatives are initially targeted to a limited audience. A successful execution of a small pilot, such as an online orientation program for a specific audience, can lead to an even bigger impact once the program is rolled out to the entire enterprise.

Table 5.3 (continued)

The McKinsey ACADEMIES Framework: Dimensions of a Strong L&D Function	
# Step	**Overview**
6. Measurement of impact on business performance	A learning strategy's execution and impact should be measured using key performance indicators (KPIs). – _Business Excellence KPI_: How closely aligned all L&D initiatives and investments are with business priorities. – _Learning Excellence KPI_: Whether learning interventions change people's behavior and performance. – _Operational Excellence KPI_: How well investments and resources in the corporate academy are used.
7. Integrate L&D into HR processes	L&D has an important role in recruitment, onboarding, performance management, promotion, workforce, and succession planning.
8. Enabling of the 70:20:10 learning framework	70% of learning takes place on the job, 20% through interaction and collaboration, and 10% through learning interventions such as classroom training.
9. Systems and learning technology applications	Significant enablers for just-in-time learning are technology platforms and applications.

Designing Cloud-Specific L&D Programs

Numerous options are available to develop and deliver cloud training programs. One option is purchasing cloud training programs and courses from third-party education vendors. Table 5.4 presents examples of such courses.

The advantage of this option is time savings and access to courses developed with input from cloud and AI experts. A major disadvantage is off-the-shelf courses may not be fully responsive to the unique attributes of an organizations and may not fully meet learner needs.

LinkedIn Learning is a useful resource that offers over 23,000 courses and is available in 24 languages. The author, David Linthicum, is a significant contributor to LinkedIn Learning since 2016, and offers 26 online courses covering topics such as Cloud Strategy, Leveraging AI Agents, Public/Private/Multicloud Options, Internet of Things, and other core cloud concepts.[113]

Organizations may also develop their own cloud-courses and programs through their in-house L&D function. The advantage of this option is courses and

Table 5.4: AI and Cloud L&D Program Topics, as Adapted from Arcitura.[112]

Arcitura Cloud Fields of Practice	Knowledge and Proficiency
Cloud Professional	Cloud computing concepts, models and business considerations, and proficiency in fundamental technology and security-related areas of cloud computing.
Cloud AI Professional	How predictive AI can be used and applied in a range of business applications.
Cloud Technology Professional	Identification, positioning and utilization of modern cloud technologies and associated security considerations.
Cloud Architect	Technology architecture that underlies cloud platforms and cloud-based IT resources and solutions, and has mastered the hands-on application of design patterns, principles and practices used to engineer and evolve such environments.
Cloud Security Specialist	Common threats and vulnerabilities associated with cloud-based environments, and in establishing security controls and countermeasures via the mastery of cloud security patterns and practices.
AI Consultant	Important aspects of predictive AI and generative AI utilization, implementation and architecture.
Cloud Governance Specialist	Defining, establishing, and evolving governance controls and frameworks specifically for cloud-based IT resources and platforms in support of organizational and technological governance requirements.
Cloud Storage Specialist	Mechanisms, devices, technologies, practices, and overall assessment criteria pertaining to cloud storage technologies and services
Cloud Virtualization Specialist	Technologies, mechanisms, platforms, and practices based upon and associated with contemporary virtualization environments and cloud-based virtualization architectures.

programs will be customized to the unique characteristics of the organization and can be modified, as necessary. Creating customized courses however is time consuming, costly, and requires access to specialized cloud technical skills and specialized skills to deliver the training.

Some organizations choose a combination of all options available to create a cloud-enabled workforce. Organizations are creatively designing and delivering L&D content using the cloud-driven Metaverse for an immersive training experience. For example, Walmart is using Augmented Reality (AR) for employee training in customer service scenarios, Boeing is using AR for aircraft assembly training, and UPS is leveraging it for driver training programs.[114] Regardless of the approach, it is essential to prioritize and integrate the people-side of cloud transformation into organizational change management strategies.

Budget Considerations

The budget considerations for a cloud adoption change management program of a medium-sized organization ranges from USD $50,000 and USD $250,000. This amount can vary based on several factors including organization size and complexity, geographic distribution of workforce, organizational culture and resistance, scope of cloud transformation, cloud maturity level, and the timeline for implementation. The common budget allocations include:

– Change management consultants: USD $30,000–100,000
– Training programs: USD $15,000–60,000
– Internal change champions: USD $20,000–50,000
– Communication tools and campaigns: USD $10,000–30,000
– Employee engagement activities: USD $5,000–20,000
– Assessment and feedback mechanisms: USD $5,000–15,000

Management could adopt a phased approach, starting with a core group of champions before expanding the program. This method allows for adjustments based on initial feedback and can help control costs while increasing engagement. Effective change management programs allocate sufficient resources for ongoing training and support beyond the initial implementation phase, recognizing cloud adoption is a continuous process, not a one-time event.

The budget considerations cloud computing learning and development program of a medium-sized organization ranges from USD $60,000 and USD $200,000 annually. This amount can vary based on several factors including the number of employees requiring training, types of cloud platforms, delivery methods (instructor-led vs. self-paced), the current and future cloud staff expertise, and required certifications. The common budget allocations include:

– Technical training subscriptions: USD $20,000–70,000
– Certification exam fees: USD $10,000–40,000
– Instructor-led training sessions: USD $15,000–50,000
– Custom learning content development: USD $10,000–30,000
– Learning management system: USD $5,000–20,000
– Skills assessment tools: USD $5,000–15,000
– Training time (productivity cost): Variable

Management could adopt a role-based training approach, focusing on cloud skills needed for different job functions. This targeted approach maximizes the return on investment while ensuring staff develop the skills most relevant to their responsibilities.

Call to Action

1. Conduct a digital skills gap analysis of the organization's current workforce and implement strategies to address staffing and competency gaps.
2. Decide which framework to implement an effective organizational change management strategy to deploy the large-scale adoption of the cloud.
3. Involve employees on planning, communicating the vision for innovation objectives, and proactively addressing automation concerns.
4. Establish clear career progression paths and decide how to deliver cloud and AI training content to employees.
5. Evaluate whether a Cloud Center of Excellence is an efficient way for the organization to manage the cloud activities across the enterprise.

Box 5.1: Role of the CIO

The AI-enabled cloud transforms the roles and skills of the in-house IT function, especially the Chief Information Officer (CIO). The CIO plays a substantial role in identifying actions necessary to harmonize the IT function with the organization's AI and cloud strategy. The CIO is no longer the IT developer of the 1980s. Figure 5.1 lists the CIO role, by decade, as adapted from Deloitte.

1980s
Developer
Establishing and
managing the
organization's IT
department and
for programming
IT infrastructures
of the
oraganization

2000s
Integrator
Increasing overall
company
performance by
both the
effectiveness of
how technology is
used and how
synergies are
created

2020s
Business savvy
Technologist
Embedding
technology in
the business
strategy for
digital
transformations

1990s
Aligner
Aligning
technology to
help the CEO to
design and
define new
business models
because Internet
became a
critical business
driver

2010s
Architect
Integrating
externally available
IT services, such as
web services from
cloud platforms,
and creating
holistic
accessibility of
available
technology

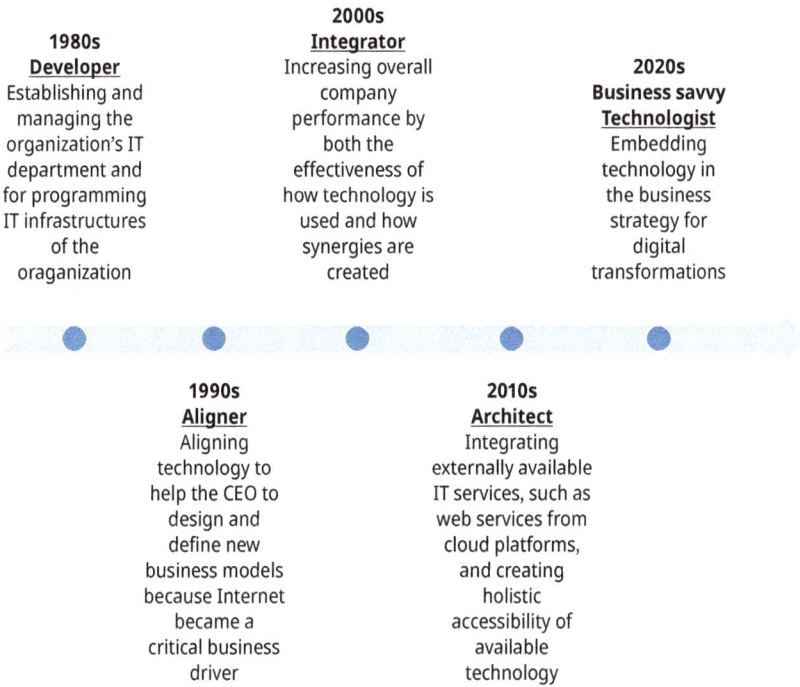

Figure 5.1: CIO Role, by Decade, as adapted from Deloitte.[115,116]

The CIO as the business savvy technologist must be able to effectively communicate with other management executives and the Board of Directors. The CIO must be able to clearly articulate how AI
and the cloud can drive business strategic outcomes without using IT jargon.

Part III: **Governance Disrupted and Transformed by the Cloud**

Chapter 6
Sharing Cloud Governance Responsibilities and Integrating the Cloud with Enterprise Risk Management

The price of greatness is responsibility.[117]
– Winston Churchill, Former Prime Minister of the United Kingdom

Introduction

The organization has overall and primary responsibility for cloud governance. This chapter discusses integrating a shared responsibility model for the organization to employ proactive cloud risk management and governance practices while engaging with CSPs. This chapter boldly illustrates what actions management should take to identify and assess the myriad of risks associated with cloud and AI.

This chapter describes the value of integrating a cloud perspective into a risk assessment to facilitate management's understanding of the cloud risks across the entire organization and ensure resiliency. Cyber resilience refers to the ability to recover quickly from cloud failures and thrive during a crisis (i.e., significant cloud breach).

What is a Cloud Shared Responsibility Model?

The cloud disrupts and transforms how technology, applications, and data are deployed, accessed, managed, and governed. *Why is that?* The primary reason for this disruption is shifting selected responsibilities from the organization's on-premises IT functions to third-party CSPs. This paradigm shift is commonly called a *cloud shared responsibility model*. This book posits cloud shared responsibility as a conceptual model that defines, divides, and allocates distinct material responsibilities for cloud governance to four cohorts of organizational stakeholders, as illustrated in Table 6.1.

Table 6.1: Stakeholders of a Cloud Shared Responsibility Model, Source: Authors.

Stakeholder	Description
1. Democratized IT employees outside of the IT function <u>authorized</u> to engage directly with the cloud and AI	Represents organizational employees outside the in-house IT function authorized to engage directly with cloud activities, including outsourcing CSP services.
	Management should define shared responsibilities with employees concerning cloud governance policies and functions (e.g., centralized IT department, compliance department, etc.). A cloud shared responsibility model would place expectations and policy requirements on each employee for cloud governance.
2. Employees outside of the IT function <u>not authorized</u> to engage in shadow cloud activities	Shadow IT activities, including cloud activities and AI use cases, represent the unauthorized and unknown use of cloud activities by organizational employees outside of the purview of the centralized IT function and organizational governance functions.
	Management should define shared responsibilities between employees and cloud governance policies and functions (e.g., centralized IT department, compliance department, etc.). A cloud shared responsibility model would place an expectation and policy requirements on each employee for cloud governance.
3. Organizational governance functions with cloud governance responsibilities	Multiple organizational governance structures are responsible for elements of IT governance. For example, the Compliance, Security, and ERM functions often coordinate and collaborate on efforts to share responsibilities for managing risks to strategic IT objectives (e.g., data privacy).
	Management must transform the organization's governance functions to account for these shared responsibilities and address the unique complexities of the cloud.
4. Third-Party Cloud Vendors (e.g., CSP)	A CSP relationship *extends the organization* outside the boundaries of the organization. According to Deloitte, "Executives extend the enterprise every time they use a cloud service, outsource a business process, or otherwise spread operations beyond the traditional four walls of their organization."[118] This paradigm is commonly referred to as the *extended organization*.

Cloud Hyperscalers like Amazon, Microsoft, and Google share similar responsibility models:

1. Division of security responsibilities between the CSP and organization, with clear delineation of who secures what aspects of the cloud environment.
2. Shared accountability for compliance, where CSPs ensure their infrastructure meets regulatory requirements, and the organization remains responsible for configuring the workloads and applications to comply with regulations and standards.
3. Provider responsibility for the underlying infrastructure security, including physical data centers, hardware, and network.
4. The organization's responsibility for securing data, including encryption, access controls, and classification of sensitive information.
5. The organization owns identity and access management, which requires proper configuration of user permissions and authentication mechanisms.

These similarities reflect the fundamental premise that effective cloud governance requires a coordinated effort between the organization and CSPs, with each party handling distinct and complementary aspects of the overall cloud security posture.

With the integration of AI capabilities, the cloud further evolves, offering enhanced automation, predictive analytics, and intelligent decision-making processes. This AI-cloud synergy amplifies the potential benefits and introduces new layers of complexity to the cloud shared responsibility model. The Cloud Security Alliance (CSA) states,

> Responsibilities for security and compliance for AI applications are shared between the AI Service User, the Enterprise (Application Owner), and the AI Service Providers. This shared responsibility model helps demarcate and provide a clear separation of duties. This enables newer AI applications to be created and deployed at a faster pace, while being secure and compliant.[119]

The Extended Enterprise Within a Cloud Shared Responsibility Model

The deployment of the cloud at scale often involves procuring services from CSPs and therefore, substantially and rapidly extends an organization. This cloud-extended organization creates a complex web of distributed, interconnected, and interdependent shared-responsibility stakeholders, including employees (i.e., first party), customers (i.e., second party), vendors, and their hired subcontractors (i.e., third, fourth, and fifth parties). Figure 6.1 depicts this web of extended relationships.

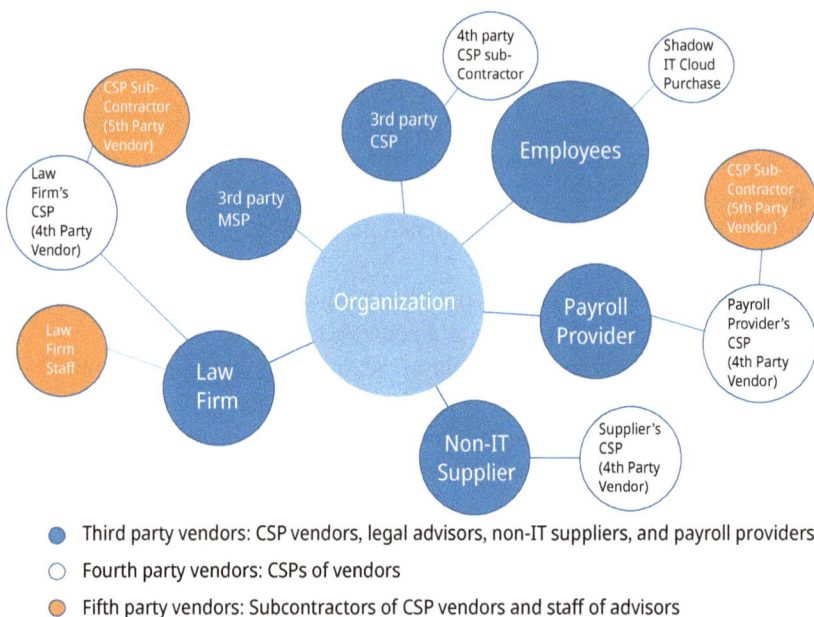

- Third party vendors: CSP vendors, legal advisors, non-IT suppliers, and payroll providers
- Fourth party vendors: CSPs of vendors
- Fifth party vendors: Subcontractors of CSP vendors and staff of advisors

Figure 6.1: Extended-Enterprise: Web of Data Sharing in the Cloud Computing Domain, Source: Authors.[120]

Both the CSP (the vendor) and the organization (the customer/buyer) are responsible for monitoring the cloud's integrity, availability, and operations. The organization – not the CSP – has the primary responsibility and will be held fully accountable by regulators and other key stakeholders for the proper operation, performance, and governance of the cloud.

Managing Cloud Risk

This cloud shared responsibility model requires a clear distinction and definition of governance and operational roles and responsibilities between the organization and key stakeholders, like CSPs, who share responsibilities with the organization. According to the CSA, "Defining the line between your responsibilities and those of your providers is imperative for reducing the risk of introducing vulnerabilities into your public, hybrid, and multi-cloud environments."[121]

The cloud provides unique and compelling opportunities that range from realized cost savings to innovation, efficiency, and improved decision-making. At the same time, the cloud creates unintended consequences, exacerbates existing risks, and creates new risks. Management needs to engage in risk management practices to address the myriad of risks associated with cloud computing. *What can management do to manage cloud risk?* The first step would be for management to identify and assess the cloud risks. Table 6.3 within the call out box describes commonly used techniques to identify risk.

Deloitte published a cloud risk map presenting their perspective on possible risks associated with cloud computing. Table 6.2 highlights examples of cloud risks by major categories of cloud strategic objectives identified by Deloitte.

Table 6.2: List of Cloud Computing Risks, as Adapted from Deloitte's Cloud Computing Risk Intelligence Map.[122]

Cloud Objective	Cloud Risk
Cloud Strategy	– Lack of a coherent cloud strategy or misalignment with other business strategies – Lack of an exit strategy for an organization or CSP – Ineffective organizational change management for cloud adoption – Lack of skills and experience to execute strategy
Cybersecurity	– Cloud misconfigurations that result in a data breach – Poor security practices by the organization – Failure to secure network traffic – Unauthorized exposure of data at cloud locations – Lack of proper isolation for sensitive data – Failure to apply security patches – Failure to implement proper access controls
Data Governance	– Failure to appropriately remove data from multiple clouds – Lack of clear ownership of cloud-generated data – Poorly designed practices can lead to poor fiscal performance, compliance, regulatory fines and penalties, and destruction of reputation and stakeholder trust
Operations	– Failure to control cloud expenses – Inadequate records management, preservation, retention, and disposal policies – Failure to consider e-discovery issues in contracts – 24/7 availability as an expectation
Compliance	– Noncompliance with data privacy laws due to cross-jurisdictional data transfer and lack of visibility into data location – Inability to demonstrate compliance with regulatory requirements – Difficulty validating continuous compliance with evolving regulations and standards

Table 6.2 (continued)

Cloud Objective	Cloud Risk
Incident Response	– Delay by the CSP in the notification or lack of notification of a data breach – Ineffective incident investigation – Lack of ability to develop an effective incident response program when the organization does not have control or access to the cloud infrastructure assets
Vendor Selection	– Inadequate due diligence to select CSP – Failure to plan for cloud portability and interoperability
Performance Management	– Lack of performance monitoring mechanisms – Interruption of cloud services due to critical subcontractor failure – Loss of direct control over and access to the cloud infrastructure. – Reliance upon contracts with terms and conditions to manage outcomes – New skills needed to manage and oversee CSP performance
Employee Learning	– Inadequate IT skills to manage cloud technologies – Insufficient staff expertise in auditing cloud environment

Additionally, there are key risks related to the AI-enabled cloud, including:
– Falling behind competitors in AI adoption and capabilities
– Lack of AI governance structures and policies
– Difficulty establishing effective oversight of AI
– Poisoned data used to train or test AI models
– Generative AI hallucinations and misinformation
– Unauthorized access that allows illegitimate users to interact with AI models
– High costs of AI implementation and maintenance for updating and retraining models
– Uncertain ROI due to AI's rapidly evolving nature
– Difficulty validating compliance with AI regulatory requirements
– False claims made by vendors about the effectiveness of their AI-enabled cloud offerings
– Insufficient enterprise capacity for AI-enabled cloud innovation
– Fail to plan for interoperability to ensure AI operates across multiple cloud environments
– Lack of transparency in AI decisions and inherent bias
– Lack of an inventory of AI use cases

Once management identifies the risks, the next step is for management to design and implement risk mitigation activities to reduce these and other cloud-AI risks to an acceptable level.

Risk mitigation activities often include a combination of accepting a risk, avoiding a risk, transferring a risk, and controlling the risk. To transfer risk, management could decide to procure a cyber insurance policy. A cyber insurance policy could offer an organization coverage for business interruptions, crisis management costs, and cyber extortion. A cyber insurance policy could also cover liabilities such as regulatory fines, penalties, and privacy breaches. Embroker, the insurance services company, calculated the insurance claim amount as a case study example for a cloud data breach.

> A software company experienced a configuration error in their cloud storage, exposing client data for 72 hours. The exposure affected 100,000 customer records across multiple clients. The cyber insurance policy covered a total of $1.3 million USD, including $500,000 USD in third-party liabilities, $300,000 USD in notification expenses, $400,000 USD in legal costs, and $100,000 USD in public relations/crisis management expenses, technology liabilities, and data-related risks.[123]

To control or mitigate a risk, management would implement internal controls activities through various business processes. COSO defines the term *control activities* as:

> Actions (generally described in policies, procedures, and standards) that help management mitigate risks to ensure the achievement of objectives. Control activities may be preventive or detective in nature and may be performed at all levels of the organization.[124]

In the context of the cloud, control activities play an essential role in cloud risk mitigation strategies designed to reduce cloud risk to an acceptable level. The Cloud Security Alliance (CSA) Cloud Controls Matrix (CCM) is an example of a framework for cloud control activities. According to the CSA, "the CCM is a cybersecurity control framework for cloud computing."[125] Table 6.6 within the call-out box presents the CSA CCM domains.

Integrating the Cloud into Enterprise Risk Management

To understand the full spectrum of cloud risks across the organization, management should leverage an enterprise risk management (ERM) framework. ERM facilitates an approach for management to integrate, communicate, and share a strategically aligned portfolio view of risk. Table 6.4 within the call-out box presents an illustrative example of a ERM risk portfolio for cloud and AI activities. Sharing this ERM portfolio amongst senior executives and the Board of Directors gives cloud risks a broader visibility across the enterprise.

The cloud shared responsibility model provides a structured approach to identifying and categorizing risks, which can be integrated into the organization's broader ERM risk profile. James Lam, a globally recognized risk expert, suggests, "It's not just about risk monitoring and reporting; it's about using risk insights and analytics to drive better business decisions. [The board needs to] understand what drives earnings, cash flows, and value."[126]

Management must proactively manage risk to avoid misinterpretation and inadequately execute the cloud's shared responsibilities. Irrespective of shared responsibility arrangements, the organization has overall and primary responsibility for cloud governance. Table 6.5 within the call-out box provides examples of ERM responsibilities that management must identify for the Board of Directors and senior executive positions and hold these cohorts accountable for their share of cloud and AI governance. Understanding the division of responsibilities can aid in more accurate risk quantification, supporting data-driven decision-making.

Budget Considerations

The budget considerations for a cloud enterprise risk management program of a medium-sized organization ranges from USD $75,000 and USD $250,000. This amount can vary based on several factors including industry regulations, cloud complexity (single vs. multi-cloud), geographic distribution of operations, and the maturity level of security and risk management programs. The common budget allocations include:

- Risk assessment and monitoring tools: USD $25,000–80,000
- Risk management personnel: USD $60,000–150,000
- Third-party risk evaluations: USD $15,000–50,000
- Risk response planning and testing: USD $10,000–30,000
- Governance documentation and reporting: USD $5,000–20,000

The most successful cloud risk programs integrate with the organization's enterprise risk management framework instead of operating in isolation. This allows for more efficient resource utilization and comprehensive risk visibility across the enterprise.

The budget considerations for a cloud shared responsibility program of a medium-sized organization ranges from USD $60,000 and USD $200,000. This amount can vary based on several factors including industry regulations, CSPs and deployment models in use, organization size and complexity, integration with existing governance frameworks, and clarity of documentation for current responsibilities. The common budget allocations include:

- Responsibility mapping and documentation: USD $15,000–40,000
- Gap assessment and remediation: USD $20,000–60,000

- Training: USD $10,000–30,000
- Control validation tools: USD $15,000–50,000
- Third-party assessments: USD $10,000–40,000
- Ongoing program management: USD $15,000–50,000

Management may implement their shared responsibility model program in stages, beginning with mapping responsibilities and performing a gap analysis, followed by control validation. This staged approach helps to manage costs and establish clear lines of accountability.

Call To Action

1. Define shared responsibilities between the CSP, organizational stakeholders, cloud governance policies and functions. Ensure roles are clearly defined to respond to risk.
2. Identify and assess the cloud risks.
3. Design and implement risk mitigation activities to reduce cloud/AI risks to an acceptable level.
4. Share the risk portfolio with management and the Board of Directors to provide broader visibility into cloud risks across the organization and enhance cloud resiliency.

Box 6.1: Risk Identification Techniques

Identifying cloud risks is a complex and iterative process. A range of techniques are available in the public domain to assist with the risk identification process. For instance, the European Network and Information Security Agency's (ENISA)[127] and the Project Management Institute[128] advance a variety of techniques that organizations can use to identify potential risks. Table 6.3 lists the commonly used risk identification techniques.

Table 6.3: Commonly Used Techniques to Identify Risk.

Risk Identification Technique	Description
Brainstorming	Bring a group together to creatively identify risks.
Delphi	Individuals separately identify risks. Then, a group of experts collectively review and finalize the list of risks.
Interviewing	Ask key stakeholders questions to help identify risks.

Table 6.3 (continued)

Risk Identification Technique	Description
Focus Groups	A facilitator guides a group discussion about risk. The group could be from the same unit or from different units of the organization.
Survey	Develop survey questions designed for stakeholders to answer questions about their area of responsibility to identify risks.
Documentation Reviews	Review documentation such as an audit report or process flow chart to identify risk.
Environmental Scanning	Analyze information about trends and relationships in an organization's internal and external environment.
Scenario Planning	According to Deloitte, "scenario planning helps organizations perceive risks and opportunities more broadly, to imagine potential futures and different scenarios that might challenge their assumptions, and to spot sources of risk that may otherwise go undetected."[129]

Box 6.2: Illustration of a Cloud and AI ERM Portfolio

Table 6.4: Example ERM Portfolio, Source: Authors.

Identify Risk	Risk Category	Assess Risk		Risk Responses	Owner
		Likelihood	Impact		
Strategic Objective: Shared-responsibility Model					
If an organization does not invest in, adequately implement, and maintain cloud computing to meet its business needs, then innovations and efficiencies in operations may not be achieved.	Strategic	Medium	High	Reduce Risk Response: – Formalize terms of cloud services with a Service Level Agreement (SLA) to document roles and shared responsibilities between the organization and CSP vendor. – Perform due diligence before entering into an agreement with a third-party CSP.	CEO CIO

Table 6.4 (continued)

Identify Risk	Risk Category	Assess Risk		Risk Responses	Owner
		Likelihood	Impact		
Organizational Culture Objective: Advance the Use of Cloud					
If stakeholders subvert the initiative to use cloud computing, then the change may not be adopted.	Strategic	Medium	Medium	Accept Risk Response: – Understand how to engage stakeholders and manage their expectations. – Assess the change readiness of stakeholders. – Communicate the importance of the change, timeframes, and responsibilities of stakeholders. – Reduce Risk Response: Develop training for stakeholders.	CEO CIO
If management does not consider the relevance, redundancy, and adequacy of the internal IT staff competencies and roles because of the cloud and AI, then the organization will lack experienced personnel, impacting cloud performance on business objectives.	Strategic	Medium	Medium	Reduce Risk Response: – Retain and upskill current staff on AI, GenAI, Agentic AI, and cloud. – Hire cloud and AI experts. – Define roles to set clear expectations about staff responsibilities because of cloud and AI adoption.	CIO CHRO

Table 6.4 (continued)

Identify Risk	Risk Category	Assess Risk		Risk Responses	Owner
		Likelihood	Impact		
Cybersecurity Objective: Safeguard Data					
If there is a failure to safeguard personally identifiable information that results in a breach/incident, then there will be an adverse impact on the business and the individuals whose information was compromised.	Operational	Low	High	<u>Reduce Risk Response</u>: Establish cybersecurity policies and procedures, conduct annual IT audits, and require employees to complete security awareness training. <u>Transfer Risk Response</u>: Invest in cyber insurance policy to cover loss and expenses arising out of a security breach.	CIO
If poisoned data is used to train or test AI models, then models may produce harmful, biased, or misleading outputs when deployed.	Operational	Medium	High	<u>Reduce Risk Response</u>: – Implement data validation, sanitization techniques, and strict access controls to prevent contamination. – Conduct audits and deploy anomaly detection to enhance resilience against poisoning attacks. – Trace data changes to identify malicious modifications.	CIO
Compliance Objective: Regulatory Requirements					
If the organization does not monitor cloud data transfers across jurisdictions, then it will not comply with data privacy laws.	Compliance	Medium	Medium	<u>Reduce Risk Response</u>: – Create and continuously update a cloud asset inventory, including locations (jurisdictions, regions, countries, states) of cloud servers. – Demonstrate compliance with regulatory requirements to auditors and stakeholders.	CEO CIO

Table 6.4 (continued)

Identify Risk	Risk Category	Assess Risk		Risk Responses	Owner
		Likelihood	Impact		
Financial Objective: Concentration of one CSP					
If the organization is unaware of a concentration of one CSP, then cost overruns may harm revenue and financial results.	Financial	Medium	Medium	Accept Risk Response: Cloud administrator actively monitors cloud usage and cost reports. Reduce Risk Response: Adjust risk appetite to consider expanding to a multi-cloud strategy.	CEO CFO CIO
Operations Objective: Increase Business Resilience					
If the organization is unaware of the full inventory of cloud services being used, critical weaknesses may go undetected, and data may be subject to theft, exploitation, and manipulation.	Operational	High	High	Reduce Risk Response: Create and continuously update a cloud asset inventory.	CEO CIO
If an SLA with CSP does not exist or does not specify terms related to data rights, data usage, or vendor lock-in, then an organization may be at risk of not efficiently managing cloud services and performance.	Operational	Medium	Medium	Reduce Risk Response: Require the CSP to provide cost calculation tools and data usage monitoring services. Document data ownership rights and the ability to retrieve data from CSP upon term-end.	CIO

Table 6.4 (continued)

Identify Risk	Risk Category	Assess Risk		Risk Responses	Owner
		Likelihood	Impact		
If an SLA with CSP does not specify terms related to oversight, accountability, and monitoring, then the organization is unaware of the adequacy of a third-party CSP's risk management practices.	Operational	High	High	Accept Risk Response: Describe the role of CSP to monitor subcontractors providing fourth-party cloud services. Define whether data stored on CSP servers must be located in the home country. Document roles, responsibilities, nature, timing, scope, and frequency of internal audit and third-party assurance.	CIO

Box 6.3: Examples of ERM responsibilities

Table 6.5: Examples of ERM responsibilities, Source: Authors.

Role	Description of Cloud-ERM Responsibilities

Governance Bodies (e.g., Board of Directors, Risk Committee)	– Have an overall understanding of cloud computing.
	 – Proactively engage management on cloud governance. For example, McKinsey recommends four ways for the Board to engage on the topic of cloud:
	   – "Link cloud to overall strategy discussion
	   – Incorporate cloud into risk and compliance discussion
	   – Support the development of cloud capabilities
	   – Oversee and communicate cloud financial impact."[130]

CEO Chief Executive Officer (CEO)	– Gain an awareness of how the industry and competitors use the cloud. – Understand the lessons learned from high-profile cloud breaches. – Define the company's risk appetite for outsourcing functions to a CSP.

Table 6.5 (continued)

Role	Description of Cloud-ERM Responsibilities
Chief Financial Officer (CFO)	– Account for implementation costs incurred in cloud computing service agreements in compliance with financial accounting standards. – Calculate cloud Return on Investment. – Monitor and manage cloud cost management (e.g., cost overruns).
Chief Information Officer (CIO)	– Lead the development and implementation of the organization's cloud strategy, cloud security posture, and cloud security controls. – Monitor the performance of CSPs related to ERM. For example, compliance with cloud laws and regulations, cyber security attacks, incident response and availability outages. – Analyze external audit reports to validate CSP cloud governance. – Mature incident response capabilities to prevent, detect, and correct cloud breaches.
Chief Audit Executive (CAE)	– Evaluate the organization's approach to managing cloud risk. – Report cloud-related internal audit results to the Board of Directors (e.g., Audit Committee of the Board). – Conduct due diligence to help management in CSP vendor selection. – Assess the maturity of the organization's vendor risk management program.
Chief Risk Officer (CRO)	– Collaborate with business units to facilitate the assessment of enterprise risks, including cloud risks. – Provide the Board of Directors, CEO, and the CAE with regular updates on the status of critical cloud risks. – The CRO function may not exist in some organizations. Sometimes, the CFO has the collateral responsibility to communicate risk to management. Some organizations, with or without a CRO, assemble a Risk Committee to oversee ERM. The Council members are typically division heads who own the risks for their respective business units.

Box 6.4: CSA CCM domains

Table 6.6: CSA CCM: Cloud Control Domains, as Adapted from the Cloud Security Alliance's Cloud Controls Matrix.[131]

Domain #	Domain of the CSA's Cloud Control Matrix	Description
1	Audit & Assurance	Includes independent audits, assurance assessments, and regulatory compliance
2	Application & Interface Security	Governs application security, as well as data integrity/access/security
3	Business Continuity Management and Operational Resilience	Relates to developing strategies for recovery from business disruptions, backing up data stored in the cloud, and preparing for disasters
4	Change Control and Configuration Management	Relates to the management of risks associated with changes to applications and systems, and the quality change control, approval, and testing process
5	Cryptography, Encryption & Key Management	Relates to defining and implementing cryptographic, encryption, and Key Management to protect, store, and access sensitive data
6	Datacenter Security	Deals with the physical security of data centers and servers
7	Data Security and Privacy Lifecycle Management	Includes the classification, protection, and handling of data throughout its lifecycle
8	Governance, Risk and Compliance	Relates to overall cloud governance, overall cloud policy exceptions, and Enterprise Risk Management
9	Human Resources	Includes employee termination, remote work policies, and IT security training
10	Identity & Access Management	Governs separation of duties, strong authentication, user access restriction, and strong passwords
11	Interoperability & Portability	Interoperability relates to communications between applications or providers Portability relates to the ability to move data/services from one provider to another
12	Infrastructure & Virtualization Security	Includes network security, secure migration to cloud environments

Table 6.6 (continued)

Domain #	Domain of the CSA's Cloud Control Matrix	Description
13	Logging and Monitoring	Deals with the security and retention of audit logs, restriction of access to audit logs, and encryption monitoring and reporting
14	Security Incident Management, E-Discovery, & Cloud Forensics	Deals with security breach notifications and incident response metrics/testing/plans
15	Cloud Supply Chain Management, Transparency, and Accountability	Includes compliance testing, applying the Shared Responsibility Model to cloud security, data quality and integrity, supply chain relationships, and contractual agreements
16	Threat & Vulnerability Management	Relates to preventive controls to protect the organization against cloud breaches such as breach detection tools, compromise assessments, and penetration testing
17	Universal Endpoint Management	Governs the proper security of third-party endpoints with access to the organization's assets and manage endpoints to prevent data loss

Chapter 7
Security, Trust, and the Cloud

Introduction

Cloud cybersecurity threats emerge with the deployment of the cloud. Organizations must protect their data, networks, infrastructure, and applications from such security threats. A comprehensive cloud security strategy, framework, controls, and an incident response plan are essential governance mechanisms to secure the cloud. Organizations are increasingly deploying artificial intelligence and machine learning technologies to detect anomalies and respond to threats in real-time, providing an additional layer of defense for cloud environments. However, organizations must also be mindful that AI itself can introduce new security vulnerabilities that attackers may attempt to exploit. *What should management know about the critical elements of cloud security?*

This chapter discusses cloud security in the context of governance, highlighting basic concepts and challenges. It explains the importance of a Zero Trust approach in a cloud security strategy. Effective security is essential for strong governance, as even minor lapses can lead to severe data breaches, compromising stakeholder confidence and resulting in significant legal and financial consequences.

Defining Cloud Security

Cloud security is part of the broader domain of IT security, also referred to as cybersecurity. NIST defines cybersecurity as,

> Prevention of damage to, protection of, and restoration of computers, electronic communications systems, electronic communications services, wire communication, and electronic communication, including information contained therein, to ensure its availability, integrity, authentication, confidentiality, and nonrepudiation.[133]

How do organizations protect their data, networks, infrastructure and applications from security threats?

IT Security Frameworks and the Cloud

IT Security frameworks foster and facilitate the design of best practice cybersecurity strategies and plans. Cybersecurity frameworks vary in degree of complexity and scope. Several cybersecurity frameworks are available for management to
use as a guide for preparing cybersecurity strategies, plans and processes customized to an organization. Such IT frameworks are designed to function as blue-
prints for building a comprehensive security program to manage cybersecurity
threats. Table 7.1 contains an overview of some cybersecurity frameworks available in the public domain.

Table 7.1: Summary of Cybersecurity Frameworks Available in the Public Domain.

Framework	Description of Cybersecurity Frameworks
ISACA's Control Objectives for Information Security and Related Technology (COBIT)[134]	Offers governance guidelines to align IT with business goals. Includes principles for aligning resources with business objectives through strategic planning, value optimization, and risk management, with control objectives guiding cloud governance.
International Standards Organization (ISO) 27000[135]	Provides requirements for an information security management system to manage the security of assets such as financial information, intellectual property, employee details or information entrusted by third parties.
	ISO/IEC 27017:2015 provides guidelines for information security controls relevant to cloud services.
United Kingdom's Information Technology Infrastructure Library (ITIL)[136]	Details practices for organizations to design, implement, operate, and manage IT services. A framework to ensure cloud governance aligns with organizational goals and delivers value to improve service quality, manage risks effectively, and optimize resource utilization.
European Union Agency for Cybersecurity (ENISA): Cloud Security Guide for Small and Medium Size Enterprises (SMEs)[137]	Identifies cloud security risks and opportunities. Provides organizations a set questions to understand the CSP's level of security.
NIST Special Publication 800–53: Security and Privacy Controls for Information Systems and Organizations[138]	Catalogs security and privacy controls for information systems and organizations. Offers public and private organizations a systemic approach to develop a set of safeguarding measures for all types of computing platforms, including general purpose computing systems, cyber-physical systems, cloud-based systems, mobile devices, and Internet of Things (IoT) devices.

Table 7.1 (continued)

Framework	Description of Cybersecurity Frameworks
NIST Cybersecurity Framework[139]	Focuses on the cybersecurity aspects of defined critical infrastructure industries in the United States.
Center for Internet Security Controls[140]	Prioritizes a set of safeguards to mitigate against system and network cyber-attacks.
HITRUST Common Security Framework[141]	Provides organizations with an approach to regulatory compliance and risk management.
The Cloud Security Alliance (CSA) Cloud Controls Matrix[142]	Provides a tool for assessing the adequacy of security and related controls when deploying cloud computing services.

Selecting a security framework will depend on the unique characteristics of an organization. For instance, laws and regulations, business needs, size, and appetite for risk. For the cloud, management may begin with selecting one of the IT security frameworks available in the public domain that most closely aligns with the organization's cloud strategy. Once management selects a framework, management will need to customize the framework to align with their unique cloud environment.

NIST published a popular cybersecurity framework designed to help organizations of all sizes with understanding and managing cybersecurity threats. While not designed specifically for the cloud, the NIST framework is used by U.S. government agencies and is popular with organizations in other industries. Table 7.2 presents the components of the NIST Cybersecurity Framework.

Table 7.2: Components of the U.S. NIST Cybersecurity Framework.[143]

NIST Security Objective	Description
Identify	Develop the organizational understanding to manage cybersecurity risk to systems, assets, data, and capabilities.
Protect	Develop and implement the appropriate safeguards to ensure delivery of critical infrastructure services.
Detect	Develop and implement the appropriate activities to identify the occurrence of a cybersecurity event.

Table 7.2 (continued)

NIST Security Objective	Description
Respond	Develop and implement the appropriate activities to take action regarding a detected cybersecurity event.
Recover	Develop and implement the appropriate activities to maintain plans for resilience and to restore any capabilities of services that were impaired due to a cybersecurity event.

It is essential for management to adopt an IT security framework because it protects the organization from cybersecurity threats and includes guidance on risks, controls, and governance.

Security Implications Unique to the Cloud

Cloud security is a challenge. *Why is that?* The cloud is unique in several respects when compared with most other technologies. The impact of such differences influences cloud cybersecurity threats and associated cloud security protocols. For instance, Table 7.3 presents examples of unique security threats created by the cloud and associated cloud security implications, as adapted from IBM.

Table 7.3: Examples of Security Threats Unique to the Cloud, as Adapted from IBM.[144]

Cloud Threat	Cloud Security Implications
Lack of Visibility	"It's easy to lose track of how your data is being accessed and by whom, since many cloud services are accessed outside of corporate networks and through third parties."
Multitenancy	"Public cloud environments house multiple client infrastructures under the same umbrella, so it's possible your hosted services can get compromised by malicious attackers as collateral damage when targeting other businesses."
Access Management and Shadow IT	"While enterprises may be able to successfully manage and restrict access points across on-premises systems, administering these same levels of restrictions can be challenging in cloud environments." "This can be dangerous for organizations that don't deploy bring-your-own device (BYOD) policies and allow unfiltered access to cloud services from any device or geolocation."

Table 7.3 (continued)

Cloud Threat	Cloud Security Implications
Compliance	"Regulatory compliance management is oftentimes a source of confusion for enterprises using public or hybrid cloud deployments." "Overall accountability for data privacy and security still rests with the enterprise, and heavy reliance on third-party solutions to manage this component can lead to costly compliance issues."
Misconfigurations	"A substantial portion of breached records can be attributed to misconfigured assets, making the inadvertent insider a key issue for cloud computing environments." "Misconfigurations can include leaving default administrative passwords in place or not creating appropriate privacy settings."

To help management mitigate the risk of these cloud threats, the CSA has created guidance to address fourteen major domains to secure the cloud. Table 7.8 within the call-out box summarizes this CSA guidance entitled, *Security Guidance for Critical Areas of Focus in Cloud Computing*.[145]

- Identify where sensitive data is located, including how it enters, flows through, and leaves information systems.
- Integrate risk analysis and management into business processes.
- Implement audit controls to record and examine system activity.
- Conduct regular reviews of system activity.
- Use authentication mechanisms to ensure only authorized access to sensitive data.
- Encrypt sensitive information in-transit and at-rest.

Leveraging AI as a Layer of Cloud Security

Management can enhance its cloud security posture by leveraging AI tools. AI can enhance cloud security through intelligent monitoring, threat detection, and automated response capabilities. Example AI use cases entail:

- Analyzing patterns in network communication
- Detecting data exfiltration attempts
- Integrating AI tools with existing security information and event management
- Preventing unauthorized uploads or downloads
- Scanning cloud infrastructure for misconfigurations

These AI-enabled cloud security enhancements represent just the beginning of a rapidly evolving technological landscape that organizations must navigate to stay protected. To implement these AI-powered security capabilities today, organizations can leverage several technologies that are listed in alphabetical order in Table 7.4.

Table 7.4: Example AI-Enabled Cloud Security Technologies, Source: Authors.

Amazon GuardDuty	Imperva Application Security
Aqua Trivy	Microsoft Defender for Cloud
Cloudflare API Gateway	Microsoft Defender for Endpoint
CrowdStrike Falcon	Okta Adaptive Multi-factor Authentication
Darktrace	Palo Alto Prisma Cloud
Google Chronicle	Splunk Enterprise Security
IBM QRadar	Thales CipherTrust
IBM Security Verify	Vectra AI Cognito

As organizations look toward the future horizon of cloud security, McKinsey predicts that in about five years, organizations will begin adopting quantum security measures. McKinsey suggests that two quantum security use cases relate to the identification of where encryption keys are stored and the automation of recycled encryption keys.[146]

Incident Response

Incident response plays a crucial role in how organizations respond to and recover from cloud cybersecurity attacks. An *incident* may include a data breach, a compromised record, a denial-of-service attack, insider threat, malware attack or network intrusion. Incident response plans are an essential component of cloud governance. It is imperative for management to adopt a credible incident response (IR) framework to govern how to respond to and correct a cybersecurity attack. An organization can customize the IR framework to the unique characteristics of their cloud.

Cloud Incident Response Framework

IR frameworks are useful in a cloud environment. However, addressing cloud incidents is different as compared to addressing incidents within traditional IT environments. To address such differences, cloud-specific incident response frameworks assist with the unique characteristics of the cloud. For example, Table 7.5 presents a summary of the Cloud Security Alliance's cloud incident response framework.[147]

Table 7.5: Cloud IR Framework, as Adapted from the Cloud Security Alliance.[148]

Phase	Overview of the Cloud Security Alliance's Cloud IR Framework
1) Preparation Establish an incident response capability so that the organization is ready to respond to incidents.	– Solid preparation can improve an incident response team's readiness and efficiency, ensuring they are sufficiently prepared in the face of threats. – A cloud incident response plan should clearly establish everyone's roles and responsibilities, including CSPs. – Organizations should consider vetting additional third-party CSPs to have quick access to resources, should they be needed in an emergency response situation.

2) Detection and Analysis
Detection, confirmation, and analysis of suspected incidents
	– Although detection and analysis may differ from one cloud environment to the other, the monitoring scope must cover the cloud management plane in addition to deployed assets. In-cloud monitoring and alerts can be leveraged to help kick off an automated response workflow.
	Questions that need to be addressed post-incident include:
	  – When did it happen?
	  – Who discovered it and how was it discovered?
	  – Have any other areas been impacted?
	  – What is the confidence level for the non-impacted zones?
	  – Has the source been discovered?
	– Incident classification scales may be helpful to gauge the severity of impact of cloud incidents (e.g., services availability).

3) Containment, Eradication, and Recovery Minimize loss, theft of information, or disruption of service, and eliminate the threat, restore services securely and timely	– When an incident is discovered, predefined containment, eradication and recovery should be executed (e.g., taking systems offline, quarantining systems, restricting connectivity). – It is of the utmost importance not to remove the threat by blind deletion as this is equivalent to destroying evidence. – The key is to be meticulous in removing any trace of malware, threats and evaluate the compromise of data loss versus service availability. – To prevent incidents from recurring, systems should be hardened and patched following an immutable infrastructure paradigm.

Table 7.5 (continued)

Phase	Overview of the Cloud Security Alliance's Cloud IR Framework
4) Post-Mortem	– Assess the incident after it occurs to better handle future incidents through the utilization of logs review, "Lessons Learned" and after-action reports, or the mitigation of exploited vulnerabilities to prevent similar incidents in the future.
5) Coordination, Information Sharing (Continuous)	– Communication between CSPs and the organization needs to be properly established, with regular updates for affected users to mitigate losses and strategize business recovery methods. – Coordinating with key partners, IR teams in other departments, law enforcement agencies on their specific roles, responsibilities greatly reinforce cloud incident response capabilities. – This communication should be set up from the start – at the planning phase – and maintained throughout the entire process.

Three Key Aspects of Cloud Incident Response

Existing IT incident response strategies and plans will be useful in a cloud environment. However, cloud incident response plans should be customized to the unique aspects of the cloud. According to the Cloud Security Alliance, "The three key aspects that set cloud incident response apart from traditional incident response processes are governance, visibility, and the shared responsibility of the cloud."[149] Table 7.6 summarizes these three aspects of cloud IR.

Defining Zero Trust in the Context of IT and Cloud Security

In the context of cloud security, embedding trust involves management implementing operational security controls (e.g., safeguard personally identifiable information) and meeting stakeholder's expectations of trust to secure the cloud. For instance, to prevent cyber threats, organizations are adopting a Zero Trust approach to cloud security. NIST states that "Zero trust assumes there is no implicit trust granted to assets or user accounts based solely on their physical or network location (i.e., local area networks versus the internet) or based on asset ownership (enterprise or personally owned)."[151]

Table 7.6: Key Aspects about Cloud IR, as Adapted from the Cloud Security Alliance.[150]

Three Aspects of Cloud IR	Overview
1) Governance	– The organization has the primary responsibility for cloud governance, including incident response. Data and applications in the cloud however reside in multiple locations, sometimes with different CSPs. Getting the various organizations together to investigate an incident is a major challenge.
	– A cloud incident response governance model therefore must be uniquely customized to integrate the organization's and the CSP's incident response strategies, plans and procedures across all CSP cloud service and deployment models.
	– In turn, governance models need to be supported by relevant service level agreements, including protocols required to customize and measure the organization's security and incident response expectations including relevant metrics and graphics.
	– Clarity of the shared responsibilities, points of contact, response times and enumerated triggered incidents are critical preparatory steps. For example, incidents associated with privacy laws and regulations in all relevant jurisdictions.
	– Cloud architecture and design should consider incident response in order to design architecture that optimize detection time; facilitate investigation techniques; and accelerate response time; to optimize containment and recoverability capabilities.
	– Organizations should perform periodic testing and assessment of such shared responsibility strategies and plans to ensure continued conformance to expectations, discovery of undocumented changes to processes, and errors in execution.
2) Visibility	– Lack of visibility in the cloud indicates that incidents that could have been resolved quickly are now at risk of escalating.
	– The cloud has the benefit of ensuring an easier, faster, cheaper and more effective incident response when leveraged properly.
	– It is important to take great care when developing IR processes and documentation, taking full advantage of cloud architectures as opposed to traditional data center models.
	– Many tools, services, and capabilities provided by CSPs greatly enhance detection, reaction, recovery and forensic abilities that are curated for, and only possible in the cloud.
	– Cloud IR has to be proactive and architected for failure throughout the process.

Table 7.6 (continued)

Three Aspects of Cloud IR	Overview
3) Shared Responsibility	– When the organization and their CSP share cloud governance responsibilities, conditions precedent to building an effective cloud incident response program and strategy are needed. – For instance, obtaining a baseline understanding of cloud activities that can be continuously monitored to detect suspicious incidents. – This will necessitate a full understanding of the nature and scope of shared responsibilities between the organization and the CSP for incident response strategy, planning and procedures.

Zero Trust represents a fundamental shift in cybersecurity based on the idea of "never trust, always verify." In contrast to traditional security models that rely on defined perimeters and implicit trust, Zero Trust demands constant validation for every user, device, and application interaction, no matter where it originates.

The core of Zero Trust involves rethinking security around identity, access, and behavior. This means every access request must pass through rigorous authentication measures, like multi-factor authentication (MFA), while continuously monitoring for anomalies. Least-privilege access ensures users and devices only obtain the permissions they absolutely need, reducing the attack surface. This is complemented by micro-segmentation, which breaks a network into smaller "zones of trust," preventing attackers from moving laterally if the perimeter is breached.

Zero Trust is particularly critical in today's hybrid, multi-cloud, and remote-work-driven environments. As organizations span public, private, and edge clouds, implicit trust leaves too many vulnerabilities exposed. Solutions like Okta (for adaptive identity and access), Zscaler (for Zero Trust network access), or Palo Alto Networks Prisma Cloud (for workload protection) are delivering this framework in real-world architectures. Ultimately, Zero Trust is a model aimed at enhancing cyber resilience in modern, borderless IT ecosystems.

Adopting a Zero Trust approach to cloud security creates a range of benefits and challenges for an organization. Table 7.7 presents perspectives from Nord-Layer, a network access security service company, about the benefits that exceed the perceived challenges of adopting a Zero Trust approach to cloud security.

If an organization does not implement Zero Trust as a strong cloud governance practice, then the organization is at risk of a ransomware or another cyber-attack that could result in breaches of data, catastrophic legal issues, and a significant loss

Table 7.7: Benefits and Challenges of Adopting a Zero Trust Approach, Source: NordLayer.[152]

Benefits of Zero Trust	Challenges of Zero Trust
1 Security extended beyond single network locations	Configuration issues with legacy tools
2 Simple collaboration with an environment-agnostic model	Excessive disruption
3 Efficient threat detection and containment	Mitigating insider threats
4 Improved user experience and employee productivity	Securing gaps from poor planning
5 Long-term network security and cost savings	
6 Greater visibility and simplified compliance	
7 Flexibility and adaptation	

of customer trust. As an example, the company formally known as Yahoo, did not invest in its cloud security infrastructure and exposed three billion Yahoo user accounts. The lack of a cloud security program created significant negative financial effects for Yahoo, including:

- The U.S. Security and Exchange Commission charged Yahoo a USD $35 million penalty for failing to make a timely disclosure of the data breach.[153]
- Yahoo had to discount their sale price to Verizon by USD $350 million because of the cybersecurity breach.[154]
- Yahoo agreed to terms of a class action settlement in the amount of USD $117 million related to the data breaches.[155]

Budget Considerations

The budget for a cloud security program of a medium-sized organization ranges from USD $275,000 to USD $800,000 annually. This budget estimate includes adopting a Zero Trust approach for cloud computing. This amount can vary based on several factors including industry requirements, data sensitivity, cloud complexity (multi-cloud, hybrid), the organization's existing security infrastructure (identity and access management capabilities), number of users and devices, staff expertise and training needs, and the geographic distribution of the workforce.

Due to regulatory requirements in the healthcare and finance sectors, cloud security budgets are typically 1.2 to 2 times higher than the standard. This is attributed to stringent compliance mandates and the sensitive nature of the data managed. Healthcare organizations, for instance, must adhere to HIPAA regulations and uphold patient confidentiality standards. Financial institutions are subject to regulatory oversight and audit requirements. Retail and manufacturing organizations generally operate within or slightly below this range, unless they handle customer data or sensitive intellectual property. The common budget allocations include:

- Identity and access management platform: USD $40,000–120,000
- Network security tools: USD $30,000–100,000
- Endpoint detection and response solutions: USD $25,000–80,000
- Security staff and Zero Trust implementation specialists: USD $80,000–200,000
- Multi-factor authentication systems: USD $15,000–40,000
- Privileged access management: USD $20,000–60,000
- Security monitoring and analytics: USD $25,000–75,000
- Training and change management: USD $15,000–30,000
- Third-party security assessments: USD $15,000–50,000
- Incident response planning: USD $10,000–30,000

Management should adjust their cloud security program budget higher or lower depending on their industry's risk profile and regulatory responsibilities because failing to invest in cloud security can lead to costly data breaches.

Call to Action

1. Use AI cloud security tools for better identification, protection, detection, response, and recovery.
2. Create a cross-functional cloud security team from IT, compliance, legal, and business units to align security with operational needs and governance requirements.
3. Review the current governance structure against this chapter's security frameworks to identify critical gaps.
4. Implement a quarterly assessment process to evaluate governance controls and technical safeguards.
5. Develop an incident response plan to clarify governance roles during security events.

Box 7.1: CSA's Cloud Security Domains
Table 7.8 summarizes Cloud Security Alliance's guidance entitled, *Security Guidance for Critical Areas of Focus in Cloud Computing.*

Table 7.8: Cloud Security Domains, as Defined in CSA's Security Guidance.[156]

Domain #	Domain Title	Description of CSA's Cloud Security Domains
1	Cloud Computing Concepts	Defines and describes cloud computing, including terminology and architectural frameworks.

Table 7.8 (continued)

Domain #	Domain Title	Description of CSA's Cloud Security Domains
2	Governance and Enterprise Risk Management	"The ability of an organization to govern and measure enterprise risk introduced by cloud computing. Items such as legal precedence for agreement breaches, ability of user organizations to adequately assess risk of a cloud provider, responsibility to protect sensitive data when both user and provider may be at fault, and how international boundaries may affect these issues."
3	Legal Issues: Contracts and Electronic Discovery	"Potential legal issues when using cloud computing. Issues touched on in this section include protection requirements for information and computer systems, security breach disclosure laws, regulatory requirements, privacy requirements, international laws, etc."
4	Compliance and Audit Management	"Maintaining and proving compliance when using cloud computing. Issues dealing with evaluating how cloud computing affects compliance with internal security policies, as well as various compliance requirements."
5	Information Governance	"Governing data that is placed in the cloud. Items surrounding the identification and control of data in the cloud, as well as compensating controls that can be used to deal with the loss of physical control when moving data to the cloud."
6	Management Plane and Business Continuity	"Securing the management plane and administrative interfaces used when accessing the cloud, including both web consoles and APIs. Ensuring business continuity for cloud deployments."
7	Infrastructure Security	"Core cloud infrastructure security, including networking, workload security, and hybrid cloud considerations."
8	Virtualization and Containers	"Virtualization security in cloud computing still follows the shared responsibility model. The cloud provider will always be responsible for securing the physical infrastructure and the virtualization platform itself. Meanwhile, the cloud customer is responsible for properly implementing the available virtualized security controls and understanding the underlying risks, based on what is implemented and managed by the cloud provider."
9	Incident Response (IR)	"Proper and adequate incident detection, response, notification, and remediation. This attempts to address items that should be in place at both provider and user levels to enable proper incident handling and forensics."

Table 7.8 (continued)

Domain #	Domain Title	Description of CSA's Cloud Security Domains
10	Application Security	"Securing application software that is running on or being developed in the cloud. This includes items such as whether it's appropriate to migrate or design an application to run in the cloud, and if so, what type of cloud platform is most appropriate (SaaS, PaaS, or IaaS)."
11	Data Security and Encryption	"Implementing data security and encryption, and ensuring scalable key management."
12	Identity, Entitlement, Access Management	"Managing identities and leveraging directory services to provide access control. The focus is on issues encountered when extending an organization's identity into the cloud."
13	Security as a Service	"Providing third-party-facilitated security assurance, incident management, compliance attestation, and identity and access oversight."
14	Related Technologies	"Established and emerging technologies with a close relationship to cloud computing, including Big Data, Internet of Things, and mobile computing."

Chapter 8
Compliance and the Cloud

> It takes less time to do things right than to explain why you did it wrong.[157]
> – Henry Wadsworth Longfellow, Poet

Introduction

Data privacy and technology-related policies, international laws and regulations are growing in number and complexity. Regulations differ by region, country, state, and industry sector. Cloud-related policies, laws, and regulations are no exception. With the rapid adoption of AI in the cloud, organizations must now also navigate an emerging landscape of AI-specific compliance requirements, including regulations around transparency and automated decision-making. These AI compliance obligations often intersect with and complement existing cloud security concepts. This chapter discusses the importance of complying with cloud-related policies, laws, and regulations, and strategies for establishing and operating cloud compliance programs.

Defining Cloud Compliance

The Society of Corporate Compliance and Ethics (SCCE) defines compliance as "adherence to the laws and regulations passed by official regulating bodies as well as general principles of ethical conduct."[158] Importantly, cloud compliance encompasses both compliance with cloud-related laws and regulations promulgated by external bodies, and compliance with internal organizational policies. The SANS Institute, a cooperative for information security thought leadership, defines *cloud compliance* as,

> the enforcement of specific regulations, standards, and best practices designed to ensure the security and privacy of data stored and processed in cloud environments. Furthermore, cloud compliance involves implementing the necessary administrative and technical controls to protect data, systems, and applications from unauthorized access, data breaches, and other security risks.[159]

The Impact of the Cloud on Organizational Compliance

A failure to comply with cloud-related laws and regulations can have detrimental financial and brand implications. According to Microsoft,

> With companies around the world shifting from on-premises IT infrastructure to cloud computing, legal and compliance professionals face new questions from their organizations about which industries are moving to the cloud, the compliance requirements and security standards that apply, and what to expect from a cloud services contract.[160]

The cloud shared responsibility model forces both the organization and CSP to comply with data protection laws or pay penalties. An example of a regulation that significantly impacts cloud computing is the General Data Protection Regulation (GDPR). In basic terms, the GDPR requires organizations to protect the public's personal data.

Promulgated by the European Union (the EU), the GDPR was designed to harmonize data privacy laws across the EU. Since 2018, the EU has been enforcing the GDPR. Most of the GDPR penalties are a result of non-compliance with general data processing principles, followed by an insufficient legal basis for processing data.[161] The largest GDPR fine occurred in 2023 against Meta Platforms Ireland, that included Facebook and WhatsApp, in the amount of 2 billion Euros.[162] Adapting cloud environments to meet regulatory requirements may require investment in specialized tools or third-party solutions. Violations can also have a negative impact on market brand and reputation. These unplanned costs strain budgets and challenge decision-makers. Therefore, as essential components of cloud governance, management must know what jurisdiction the data in the cloud resides, as well as ensure the existence of a comprehensive and effective cloud compliance program.

To help mitigate the risk of non-compliance with the GDPR, the European Data Protection Board endorsed an EU Cloud Code of Conduct that provides guidance for CSPs to meet the obligations of GDPR Article 28. Management should examine whether their CSPs meet the Code. Table 8.1 outlines the three levels of compliance to the Code.

To further reduce the risk of non-compliance with cloud-related policy, laws, and regulations, an organization can leverage AI solutions. AI can analyze large data sets and identify misconfigurations and anomalies quickly that may indicate an area of cloud non-compliance. To improve the accuracy of identifying compliance breaches and deviations from security policies, AI can automate compliance checks and generate reports for management to expeditiously take corrective action.

Table 8.1: Three Levels of Compliance of the EU Cloud of Conduct, Source: EU COC.[163]

Level of Compliance	Description
Level 1	The CSP has performed an internal review and documented its implemented measures proving compliance with the requirements of the Code with regard to the declared Cloud Service and confirms that the Cloud Service fully complies with the requirements.
Level 2	Additional to the "First Level of Compliance", Compliance with the Code is partially supported by independent third-party certificates and audits, which the CSP has undergone with specific relevance to the Cloud Service declared adherent and which were based upon internationally recognized standards procedures.
Level 3	Identical to the "Second Level of Compliance" but Compliance is fully supported by independent third-party certificates and audits, which the CSP has undergone with regard to the Cloud Service declared adherent and which were based upon internationally recognized standards.

Compliance Programs for Multi-Cloud and Hybrid Cloud Deployment Models

Multi-cloud and hybrid cloud models complicate compliance because the organization is using different platforms that were not necessarily designed to seamlessly work together. Multi-cloud focuses on using multiple public cloud providers, while hybrid cloud involves a mix of public cloud with private/on-premises infrastructure. Both approaches introduce complexity in terms of governance, security, and compliance because each environment operates with different tools, interfaces, and security models.

It is imperative for management to align their security and compliance policies with each cloud deployment model. Tata Communications suggests best practices for multi-cloud compliance, as described in Table 8.2.

Management should document policies with sufficient detail. For consistent protection in a hybrid cloud, management should enforce compliance policies directly on workloads.

Identifying and Cataloging Cloud Compliance Requirements

Identifying and cataloging cloud-related policy, laws, and regulations compliance requirements is an essential foundational step for effective cloud compliance.

Table 8.2: Example Compliance Best Practices, Source: Tata Communications.[164]

Best Practice	Description
Standardize Policies Across Multiple Clouds	Implement uniform policies across platforms. Uniform policies reduce complexity and minimize the risk of compliance breaches.
Document Multi-Cloud Operations and Policies	Thorough documentation of multi-cloud operations and policies is essential for maintaining clarity and consistency. Documenting cloud architectures, processes, and compliance measures ensures all stakeholders have clear guidelines to make informed decisions.
Centralize Visibility with Cloud Management Platforms	Improve operational visibility by integrating data from various clouds into a single dashboard, enabling real-time analytics and proactive management. This centralized approach quickly detects and addresses compliance anomalies.
Secure Multi-Cloud Environments with Robust Security Protocols	Enforce comprehensive security measures consistently across cloud platforms. Integrate advanced security solutions that provide continuous monitoring, threat detection, and automated response mechanisms. Conduct vulnerability inspections and penetration testing to evaluate cloud environments against potential breaches. Utilize Security Information and Event Management systems to promote proactive management of security events.

The process for cataloging compliance requirements should include the following,

- Identifying, understanding, and communicating the portfolio of compliance requirements.
  This involves engaging appropriately skilled professionals to identify, understand, and communicate the nature and compliance requirements associated with a global portfolio of all applicable external laws and regulations. This portfolio should include internal ethics and governance policies.
- Cataloging and prioritizing the portfolio of compliance requirements.
  Management must answer the questions, *what is the compliance requirement* and *where in my operations globally does it apply?* An organization can catalog and prioritize by geographic region, by function, by external laws, and by internal policies. Management must continuously update this catalog.

With respect to identifying and cataloguing external laws, regulations and guidance, an organization must identify all relevant international compliance requirements. Table 8.3 presents selected examples of international laws, regulations, and guidelines with cloud and AI implications.

Table 8.3: Examples of Laws, Regulations and Guidelines with Cloud Implications.

Regulations	Region	Description
General Data Protection Regulation (GDPR)[165]	European Union	GDPR in the EU and UK Regulates the use of personal data of residents within the European Union and United Kingdom and provides rights to exercise control over resident's data. While not prescriptive, the GDPR does set out measures and principles that organizations must follow to be compliant.
Artificial Intelligence (AI) Act	European Union	"To improve the functioning of the internal market by laying down a uniform legal framework in particular for the development, the placing on the market, the putting into service and the use of AI systems in the Union, in accordance with Union values, to promote the uptake of human centric and trustworthy AI while ensuring a high level of protection of health, safety, fundamental rights . . ."[166]
Other Privacy Regulations in the EU	European Union	Within the EU, each member state may have legal requirements beyond GDPR that includes the need for personal data to be processed fairly and lawfully, to be accurate and up-to-date, "to have measures in place against accidental loss or destruction and for personal data only to be transferred to countries with adequate levels of data protection in place."[167]
Organization for Economic Co-operation and Development (OECD) Anti-Corruption Ethics and Compliance Handbook for Business[168]	International	Developed by companies, for companies, with assistance from the OECD, the United Nations Office on Drugs and Crime, and the World Bank. A source for companies' compliance program guidance.

Table 8.3 (continued)

Regulations	Region	Description
Personal Information Protection and Electronic Documents Act (PIPED Act)[169]	Canada	Relates to data privacy, governing how private sector organizations collect, use, and disclose personal information in the course of commercial business.
Health Insurance Portability and Accountability Act (HIPAA)[170]	United States	A U.S. Federal regulation designed to ensure the security and privacy of Protected Healthcare Information.
Payment Card Industry Data Security Standard (PCI DSS)[171]	United States	Companies that handle cardholder information (e.g., debit, credit, prepaid, ATM and point of sale card) are required to comply with this standard. Includes twelve major rules to protect cardholder data.
Sarbanes-Oxley Act (SOX)[172]	United States	Establishes standards for all U.S. publicly traded companies to protect shareholders and the public from accounting errors and fraud. SOX is not specific to cloud computing, but the regulation does cover IT security controls because data integrity is integral to financial reporting.
Gramm-Leach-Bliley Act (GLBA)[173]	United States	Mandates that all institutions who offer financial products or services to consumers must develop, implement and maintain comprehensive information security programs. The Act protects the confidentiality and integrity of customer records.
Federal Information Security and Management Act (FISMA)[174]	United States	Applies to all U.S. government agencies and affiliated companies that collect and process data on behalf of government agencies. The Act provides guidelines on security controls, user access, identity management, risk assessment, auditing and monitoring.
Department of Justice (DOJ) Evaluation of Corporate Compliance Programs[175]	United States	Provides guidance on how prosecutors should evaluate the effectiveness of a compliance and ethics programs in the context of plea and sentencing determinations.

Table 8.3 (continued)

Regulations	Region	Description
NASDAQ Exchange Corporate Governance Rules[176]	United States	Requires that listed companies adopt and disclose a code of business conduct and ethics to all directors, officers, and employees. Each Company shall adopt a code of conduct applicable to all directors, officers and employees, which shall be publicly available.
New York Stock Exchange[177]	United States	The NYSE rules recommend that codes address: (i) conflicts of interest; (ii) corporate opportunities; (iii) confidentiality; (iv) fair dealing; (v) protection and proper use of company assets; (vi) compliance with laws, rules, and regulations, including insider trading laws; and (vii) reporting illegal or unethical behavior.
U.S. National Institute of Standards and Technology (NIST) AI Risk Management Framework	United States	"To help individuals, organizations, and society manage AI's many risks and promote trustworthy development and responsible use of AI systems."[178] NIST prepared the Framework because of the *U.S. National Artificial Intelligence Initiative Act of 2020*.[179] To accompany this Framework, NIST published a *Playbook*[180] and the *AI Risk Management Framework: Generative AI Profile*.[181]

Globally, regulators are deciding what laws, regulations, policies, and guidelines should be in place to ensure AI is developed and deployed in a responsible manner to protect the rights and safety of the public. Annually, Stanford University publishes the AI Index Report. The AI Index provides an overview of the AI-related policy events.[182] These policy developments have profound implications for CSPs, who must navigate an increasingly complex web of international compliance requirements while maintaining the agility to innovate. Organizations utilizing cloud-based AI solutions must therefore implement robust governance frameworks that can adapt to this evolving regulatory landscape while ensuring consistent compliance across different jurisdictions.

Cloud Compliance Frameworks and Programs

A cloud compliance program is crucial for an organization's cloud governance strategy. Examples include ISO's IEC 27017, ISACA's COBIT, and CSA's STAR frameworks, which are discussed in the Security chapter. Investopedia defines a compliance program as a,

> Company's set of internal policies and procedures put into place in order to comply with laws, rules, and regulations or to uphold the business's reputation. A compliance team examines the rules set forth by government bodies, creates a compliance program, implements it throughout the company, and enforces adherence to the program.[183]

A range of publicly available compliance frameworks often serve as a helpful guide for creating a cloud compliance program. For example, the U.S. Federal Sentencing Guidelines (USFSG).

The USFSG framework is required to be implemented by all organizations convicted of federal criminal offenses promulgated by the U.S. Sentencing Commission. This compliance framework however is also used by many enterprises and government agencies as a best practices benchmark for creating or evaluating a range of compliance and ethics programs.

Importantly, the USFSG acknowledges that there is no standard, or one-size-fits-all compliance program. Instead, a compliance program must be customized to the unique attributes and compliance requirements of the organization. The USFSG however does advance two primary elements of all effective compliance programs:

(1) exercising due diligence to prevent and detect criminal activities; and

(2) creating and facilitating a culture that encourages ethical conduct and a commitment to compliance with the law.

The USFSG also defines the eight essential elements of a compliance and ethics program, as presented in Table 8.4.

Table 8.4: Essential Elements of Compliance and Ethics Programs, as Adapted from the USFSG.[184]

Essential Elements of an Effective Compliance and Ethics Program
1. Standards and procedures
2. Governance, oversight, and authority
3. Due diligence in delegation of authority
4. Communication and training

Table 8.4 (continued)

Essential Elements of an Effective Compliance and Ethics Program
5. Monitoring, auditing, and reporting systems
6. Incentives and enforcement
7. Response to wrongdoing
8. Periodically assess the risk of noncompliance and continually look for ways to improve their Compliance and Ethics Programs.

Crucially, a code of ethical conduct should be an integral component of all compliance programs, including cloud compliance programs. For instance, the U.S. NYSE and NASDAQ have rules that mandate that listed companies adopt codes of business conduct and ethics.

Cloud Compliance and Shared Responsibilities

The shared responsibilities that result from the use of CSPs disrupts and transforms existing organizational governance protocols. Management within the organization has primary responsible for cloud compliance and shares some of these cloud compliance responsibilities with CSPs outside the organization. Shared responsibility models are necessary to define shared roles and responsibilities for governing cloud compliance. For instance, management should have service level agreements in place to include requirements imposed on CSPs for cloud-related compliance policies, data gathering, controls, auditing, monitoring, and reporting. The organization should conduct periodic compliance audits and assessments, which identify opportunities to improve internal controls and ensure the organization is compliant external and internal requirements.

Once management operationalizes shared-responsibility models, an organization needs to establish a continuous process to monitor cloud compliance. The process of monitoring confirms that all parties are fulfilling their respective compliance responsibilities and to identify and respond to compliance violations.

As part of this shared responsibility model, employees also have a role to maintain cloud compliance. When employees use unsanctioned cloud services and other unapproved software, known as Shadow IT, it poses risk of compliance violations and cyber breaches for the organization. For example, a hacker could exfiltrate consumer data from an employee's vulnerable Shadow IT device, resulting in non-compliance with the GDPR. Or, an employee could carelessly input sensitive patient data into a publicly available GenAI tool and violate HIPPA regulations.

Management should employ proactive risk management practices to ensure employees maintain cloud compliance. First, management should raise employee awareness with cybersecurity training and communicate policy that describe the dangers of Shadow IT. The policy would set expectations about which cloud activities are authorized, approved, and prohibited.

- Authorized and Approved: Applications, automated tools, and software vetted and endorsed by the organization's centralized IT function
- Prohibited: High-risk applications and software that lacks security controls that may introduce malware, ransomware, or other threats to the network

Second, management should deploy an asset discovery tool to assist in the identification of cloud activity across the enterprise. Asset discovery tools can help management monitor when new, risky, and high volumes of cloud services are being used.

To cast a wider net, management can also implement a Cloud Access Security Broker (CASB). Gartner coined the term CASB and defined it as "on-premises, or cloud-based security policy enforcement points, placed between cloud service consumers and CSPs to combine and interject enterprise security policies as the cloud-based resources are accessed."[185] A CASB can help management monitor network traffic to minimize cloud data leaks and enforce cloud compliance. Table 8.5 describes the four types of primary services provided by a CASB, as adapted from the Cloud Security Alliance.[186]

Table 8.5: Primary Security Services Provided by CASBs. Source: Cloud Security Alliance.

Primary Types of CASB Services	Definition of CASB Services
Visibility	Identifies all the cloud services (both sanctioned and unsanctioned) used by an organization's employees.
Data Security	Enforces data security policies and monitors user activity to help prevent the unsafe or inappropriate sharing, transfer, or use of sensitive data.
Threat Protection	Protects cloud services from unwanted users or applications. Monitors events to identify irregular behavior, permission violations, or configuration changes that indicate a compromised account.
Compliance	Enforces real-time cloud compliance with regulations like GDPR, SOX, and HIPAA, and offers policy controls and remediation. Provides historical event data for compliance auditing.

Budget Considerations

The budget considerations for a cloud compliance program of a medium-sized organization ranges from USD $50,000 to USD $250,000 annually. This amount can vary based on several factors including industry regulations, cloud complexity (multi-cloud, hybrid), the organization's existing security and compliance infrastructure, geography scope of operations, staff expertise, and training needs. The common budget allocations include:

–   Compliance automation tools: USD $15,000–75,000
–   Third-party assessments/audits: USD $20,000–60,000
–   Staff: USD $50,000–120,000
–   Training programs: USD $5,000–25,000
–   Remediation costs: Variable

Management could initially concentrate on the most critical compliance requirements and subsequently broaden the program incrementally. This phased implementation strategy will help streamline costs, transforming the compliance initiative from an expense to a strategic investment.

Call to Action

1.   Identify and catalog cloud-related policy, laws, and regulations compliance requirements against the organization's cloud environment to find gaps.
2.   Use an asset discovery tool to detect Shadow IT.
3.   Automate compliance monitoring for real-time visibility.
4.   Develop a compliance training program for all stakeholders on cloud regulations.

Chapter 9
Audit, Assurance, and the Cloud

> We all need people who will give us feedback. That's how we improve.[187]
> – Bill Gates, Co-Founder of Microsoft and Philanthropist

Introduction

Prior to the proliferation of the cloud, internal auditors had a longstanding legacy of responsibilities associated with systems and technology owned and operated by the organization. The cloud has dramatically changed this paradigm. *Why is that?* Adopting the cloud, particularly with AI integrated into the cloud, creates a range of disruptive and transformational organizational changes in many cases.

As organizations increasingly integrate new and complex technologies into their cloud applications, boards of directors and regulators ask new questions about what roles internal and external audits should play in the technology domain. This chapter explores the roles of internal and third-party external audits in the cloud.

What Role Should *Internal Audit* Play in the Cloud?

Internal audit can play a vital role in the deployment and governance of the cloud. A big question that emerges for the board of directors and senior management is: *What is the role of internal audit with respect to the cloud?* The answer will vary by organization size, structure, country, and jurisdiction.

Internal audit's role can contribute to strong cloud governance and organizational resilience. It can span a range of responsibilities such as:
– assessing cloud strategy
– evaluating CSP vendor selections
– monitoring service level agreements with CSPs
– identifying enterprise cloud risks
– evaluating controls over cloud operations, security, and compliance

One of the biggest changes is migrating in-house data, technology, and applications outside the organization's protective boundaries to a CSP vendor. The effect of transformative technologies such as AI and machine learning also changes the traditional role served by the internal audit function. In a recent Institute of Internal Auditors (IIA) survey, seven thousand internal audit practitioners and stakeholders . . . "identified technology as the single driver that will have the greatest impact on internal audit in the next 10 years." With respect to AI, "AI will add value by enabling the analysis of more information and the development of more in-depth insights."[188]

Internal audit can leverage AI to conduct audits more effectively and efficiently. KPMG identified five ways internal audit can leverage AI:

1. "AI enhances fraud detection by analyzing extensive financial data.
2. Risk assessment is advanced by providing deeper insights.
3. Continuous auditing benefits from AI through early issue identification.
4. Audit planning is improved with automated risk evaluations.
5. Routine internal audit tasks are automated to increase efficiency using AI."[189]

Table 9.1 provides examples how AI can transform the internal audit function to be effective and efficient.

Table 9.1: Examples of How Internal Audit Can Leverage AI, Source: Authors.

Phase of Audit	Internal Audit Activity
Audit Planning and Continuous Monitoring	– Replace manual sampling with AI-powered analysis of all transactions – Identify patterns, anomalies, and control breakdowns in real-time – Flag unusual transactions for immediate investigation – Continuously monitor key risk indicators
Risk Assessment	– Use Machine Learning to analyze historical audit findings and control failures to identify high risk cloud areas to audit – Deploy AI tools to identify cloud misconfigurations – Validate disaster recovery procedures
Audit Testing	– Automate routine testing procedures such as data validation and cloud security controls – Use Natural Language Processing to analyze cloud contracts and cloud policies – Use Machine Learning to analyze cloud spend patterns and security logs – Deploy Machine Learning to identify security vulnerabilities, flag cost inefficiencies, and detect cloud compliance violations
Reporting and Audit Follow-up	– Create draft reports to communicate cloud audit findings – Automate the tracking of remediation efforts to improve cloud processes and conduct audit follow-up – Generate dashboards of cloud risks, controls, and audit findings

Internal audits of the cloud provide transparency about the organization's and CSP's risk mitigation measures. Regular audits strengthen cloud security, reduce risk, ensure regulatory compliance, and identify cloud vulnerabilities that enable management to take swift action.

What Role Should *External Audit* Play in the Cloud?

Third-party assurance services rely on specialists, such as public accounting firms, to provide professional assessments, opinions, and assurance over a range of audit and attestation objectives. Third-party assurance services help organizations reinforce their defenses against AI and cloud risks to build trust amongst decision-makers. Organizations can also leverage the specialized skills of third-party assurance providers that may not exist in-house.

However, limitations exist when using third-party assurance providers. For example, the *point-in-time* nature of assurance. That is, most cloud assurance services do not continuously assess cloud activities on a daily, minute-by-minute basis. Therefore, the assurance provided is limited to the point in time the assurance procedures were conducted. The assurance cannot be projected beyond that point. Given the velocity of change of the AI-enabled cloud, this point-in-time assurance reduces the usefulness of findings.

Information Technology (IT) Assurance Services

A wide range of services are associated with IT Assurance. For instance, assurance over the adequacy, priority, design, and operating effectiveness of *general controls* over the IT operating environment, *application-level controls* over digital applications, and third-party system and organization controls. *General-level controls* include physical hardware, data security, and computer operations controls. IT assurance may also focus on *technology application-level controls* that attempt to control data risk by mitigating unauthorized applications from executing.

Assurance services may focus on completeness and validity controls, identification, authentication, authorization verification, and/or data input controls. For instance, the American Institute of CPAs (AICPA) offers a System and Organization Controls (SOC) suite. Table 9.2 presents an overview of the three categories of AICPA SOC frameworks.

Organizations can choose to a new type of SOC assessment report, called a SOC 2+ that considers AI risks. The SOC 2+ assurance tests 38 additional controls prescribed in the International Standard Organization (ISO) 42001. "It addresses

Table 9.2: Overview of AICPA-SOC for Service Organization Frameworks.[190]

System and Organization Controls (SOC) Framework	Overview
SOC 1 SOC for Service Organizations: Report on Internal Controls Over Financial Reporting (ICFR)	Auditing *user entities'* financial statements to evaluate the effect on the user financial statements of the controls at the *third-party service organization.* For example, a payroll processor would be the third-party service organization, and company ABC, which uses the payroll processor to process its payroll, would be the user entity.
SOC 2 SOC for Service Organizations: Trust Services Criteria	These reports are intended to provide information and assurance about the controls at a service organization relevant to the *security, availability*, and *processing integrity* of the systems the service organization uses to process users' data and the *confidentiality* and privacy of the information these systems process. These reports can play an essential role in: – Oversight of the organization – Vendor management programs – Internal corporate governance and risk management – Regulatory oversight
SOC 3 SOC for Service Organizations: Trust Services Criteria for General Use Report	These reports are designed to meet the needs of users who need assurance about the controls at a service organization relevant to security, availability, processing integrity, confidentiality, or privacy *but do not have the need for or the knowledge necessary to make effective use of a SOC 2 Report.*

the unique challenges AI poses, such as ethical considerations, transparency, and continuous learning. It is designed for entities providing or utilizing AI-based products or services, ensuring responsible development and use of AI systems."[191]

Several factors will inform management's decisions on how best to deploy third-party assurance. For instance, according to Compass IT Compliance,

> These [SOC 2 Trusted Services Criteria] are particularly relevant for AI platforms, which must ensure that data is protected from unauthorized access (security), available when needed (availability), accurately processed (processing integrity), kept confidential (confidentiality), and managed in accordance with privacy laws and regulations (privacy). For AI platforms, SOC 2 compliance signals to clients that the platform has robust controls in place to manage and protect the data it processes.[192]

Cloud Assurance Frameworks

In addition to the AICPA-SOC for the U.S., the European Union (EU) Agency for Cybersecurity (ENISA) is focused on achieving a high-level and common level of cybersecurity across the EU. Table 9.3 presents the ENISA cloud assurance, AI, and governance frameworks.

Table 9.3: Examples of ENISA Cloud Assurance Frameworks.

ENISA Cloud Assurance Framework	Overview
Cloud Computing Information Assurance Framework[193]	Assurance criteria are designed to assess the risk of cloud services, compare different CSP offers, obtain assurance from selected cloud providers, and reduce the assurance burden on cloud providers.
Cloud Risk Assessment Framework[194]	An IT security guide for potential and existing users of cloud computing to inform an assessment of the security risks and benefits.
Security and Resilience in Government Clouds Framework[195]	A decision-making model that can be used to determine how operational, legal, information security requirements, budget, and time constraints can drive the identification of the architectural solution that best suits the organization.
Managing Security through SLAs Framework[196]	A framework for how to manage the security aspects of service contracts to optimize information security. The work of an organization's IT officer is evolving from exclusively setting up hardware and installing and configuring software to more time managing service contracts with IT service providers.
Multilayer Framework for Good Cybersecurity Practices for AI[197]	A scalable framework to guide National Cybersecurity Certification Authorities (NCAs) and AI stakeholders on the steps to follow to secure AI systems, operations and processes by using existing knowledge and best practices and identifying missing elements. The framework consists of three layers (cybersecurity foundations, AI-specific cybersecurity and sector-specific cybersecurity for AI).

The Information Systems Audit and Control Association (ISACA) offers a range of cloud security-related research, education, certification, events, and products. Table 9.4 presents examples of ISACA-related assurance frameworks.

Table 9.4: Examples of ISACA Cloud Assurance Frameworks.

ISACA Cloud Assurance Framework	Overview
On-premises versus Cloud Auditing[198]	A framework of considerations for auditing in a cloud environment, including the optimization of cloud audit management.
Cloud Computing Management Audit Program[199]	A customizable framework for conducting an assessment of the effectiveness of the cloud computing service provider's internal controls and security, identifying internal control deficiencies within the customer organization and its interface with the service provider and providing audit stakeholders with an assessment of the quality of and their ability to rely upon the service provider's attestations regarding controls.
Control Objectives for IT (COBIT) Framework[200]	A framework for assessing the cloud, including its associated security risks and questions about the governance and management of cloud computing.

Third-party assurance providers can be instrumental in facilitating reporting disclosures. For example, in 2023, the U.S. Securities and Exchange Commission (SEC) issued regulations requiring public companies to disclose in Form 8-K material cybersecurity incidents disclosure of cybersecurity risk management. The SEC mandates governance disclosures in Form 10-K.

Budget Considerations

The budget for a cloud audit and assurance program of a medium-sized organization ranges from USD $80,000 to USD $250,000 annually. This amount can vary based on several factors including industry requirements, cloud complexity (multi-cloud, hybrid), the organization's internal audit capabilities vs. third-party reliance, maturity of internal controls and documentation, frequency and depth of audits, and scope of cloud services requiring assessment.

The common budget allocations include:

- Third-party audit/attestation services: USD $30,000–100,000
- Audit automation and continuous monitoring solutions: USD $20,000–70,000
- Internal audit staff: USD $50,000–100,000
- Evidence collection and management systems: USD $10,000–30,000
- Remediation of identified gaps: USD $15,000–50,000
- Training on audit requirements: USD $5,000–15,000

Management could adopt a risk-based approach, focusing on higher risk cloud environments and critical compliance requirements before expanding the program's scope. Organizations with an established cloud compliance program can achieve cost efficiencies through continuous monitoring and automated evidence collection. This approach reduces the manual effort required for periodic audits.

Call to Action

1. Explore AI use cases that can transform the internal audits over cloud activities.
2. Request that internal audit assess the effectiveness of the organization's cloud strategy, evaluation of CSP vendor selection, completeness of service level agreements, and key risks and controls over cloud operations, security, and compliance.
3. Share internal and external audit reports with the Board of Directors.
4. Commission a SOC 2+ report to help ensure the organization is responsible in the development and use of AI.
5. Select an assurance framework and assess the effectiveness of the CSP. Identify missing elements and analyze whether the CSP is effectively addressing control deficiencies.

Chapter 10
The Board of Directors: Asking the Right Questions about AI and the Cloud

As organizations increasingly grapple with digital transformations, large technology invest-
ments, and shifts to the cloud, these issues regularly appear on board agendas.[201]
– McKinsey

Introduction

The Board of Directors (Board) plays a crucial role in organizational governance, including cloud governance. Boards are essential to guiding an organization's future,
ensuring its resilience, and maintaining focus on its mission and goals. The Board
must ask insightful questions and integrate risk management into its decision-
making processes. Management is accountable for executing the operations under
the high-level direction and guidance of the Board. Management must ensure that
the Board has the necessary technical expertise to advise the organization on digital
transformation. This chapter explores the Board's role and presents examples of
questions the Board may have for management about AI and the cloud governance.

Cloud Governance and the Board of Directors

The digital transformation has driven the rapid, wide-scale deployment of technologies. Boards that choose to ignore or minimize the importance of their digital
transformation oversight responsibilities do so at their own peril. According to
McKinsey, the current continued escalation in large scale adoption of the cloud is
a high priority topic on board agendas.

> The massive shift to virtual work and the great migration of consumers to digital channels
> has put digital transformations at the top of the corporate agenda and has increased attention
> on cloud's role in accelerating that process. That increased attention has tended to gravitate
> toward risk. Some boards of companies with multinational footprints, for example, harbor
> concerns around their ability to meet the regulatory requirements of different jurisdictions.
> This has led to greater board engagement on how cloud transitions may impact compliance
> and risk management, even as directors remain cautious about encroaching on or hindering
> management's responsibilities. In general, directors voiced a desire to become more fluent in
> making cloud a core part of corporate strategy discussion and development.[202]

In this context, the Board must address a range of responsibilities concerning cloud governance. The call out box at the end of the chapter discusses the Board's fiduciary responsibilities with important cloud implications.

Digital Literacy and Fluency: Is the Board *Fit-for-Purpose*?

The Oxford University Press defines the term *fit for purpose* as, "[of an institution, facility, etc.] well equipped or well suited for its designated role or purpose. Quality is inextricably linked with being fit for purpose."[203] Management's first step to ensure Board members are Fit-for-Purpose is ensuring Boards have the technical expertise in cloud computing and AI. Several market survey results suggest that some Boards lack the technical expertise to provide advice and oversight to management. For instance, in a 2023 survey titled, *Board Effectiveness: A Survey of the C-suite,* PwC and The Conference Board reported, "Only 28% of executives feel their boards are armed with the right combination of skills and expertise."[204] *What actions can management implement to help ensure that the Board is Fit-for-Purpose, literate, and fluent about technology?* Table 10.1 lists actions that management can take to strengthen Board oversight.

Table 10.1: Actions to Strengthen Board Oversight, as Adapted from Deloitte.[205]

Call to Action	Description
Finding opportunities for education to fill gaps in knowledge	What training and educational opportunities are available to help the board upskill on AI and emerging technologies? Would the board benefit from bringing in internal or external experts to inform discussions?
Reevaluating the skills matrix	Does board composition need to be adjusted to recruit board members with more experience with AI and emerging technologies? What about in the C-suite?
Revamping succession plans to be more tech-forward	Have succession plans for the board and management been updated to focus on leaders who have experience with emerging technologies, including AI? Have learning opportunities been developed to help the pipeline of future leaders expand their skills and expertise in these technologies?
Staying in the flow of action	How can the board ensure it remains actively engaged in the evolving landscape of AI, guarding against complacency and outdated perspectives and remaining agile and responsive to AI's evolving capabilities?

It is management's responsibility to continuously increase Board fluency through training and other interventions for members to understand the role AI and the cloud have in accelerating digital transformations. Management should limit using cloud-jargon when raising the Board's awareness about technology.

Digital literacy skills and fluency are important elements of the Board's responsibilities to proactively engage in AI and cloud governance. To position the Board for success, management could also explore recruiting new Board members with AI and cloud experience.

Is the Board Asking the Right Questions about the Cloud?

The Board must scrutinize the implications of AI and the cloud on the organization's strategy. To do so, the Board must effectively engage by asking the right questions. *What are the right questions board members should ask*? This section presents examples of questions Board members may ask concerning cloud governance. This is not a complete list of questions. Moreover, such questions would need to be customized to the organization. Table 10.2 presents Google Cloud's suggested questions the Board may ask concerning the cloud governance.

Table 10.2: Questions from the Board on Cloud Governance, as Adapted from Google Cloud.[206]

Questions the Board Should Consider Concerning Cloud Governance
1. How is the use of cloud technology being governed within the organization? Is clear accountability assigned and is there clarity of responsibility in decision making structures?
2. How well does the use of cloud technology align with, and support, the technology and data strategy for the organization, and, ideally, the overarching business strategy, in order that the cloud approach can be tailored to achieve those right outcomes?
3. Is there a clear technical and architectural approach for the use of cloud, that incorporates the controls necessary to ensure that infrastructure and applications are deployed and maintained in a secure state?
4. Has a skills and capabilities assessment been conducted, in order to determine what investments are needed across the organization?
5. How is the organization structure and operating model evolving to both fully leverage cloud, but also to increase the likelihood of a secure and compliant adoption?
6. How are risk and control frameworks being adjusted, with an emphasis on understanding how the organization's risk profile is changing and how the organization is staying within risk appetite?

Table 10.2 (continued)

Questions the Board Should Consider Concerning Cloud Governance
7. How are independent risk and audit functions adjusting their approach in light of the organization's adoption of cloud?
8. How are regulators and other authorities being engaged, in order to keep them informed and abreast of the organization's strategy and of the plans for the migration of specific business processes and data sets?
9. How is the organization prioritizing resourcing to enable the adoption of cloud, but also to maintain adequate focus on managing existing and legacy technologies?
10. Is the organization consuming and adopting the cloud provider's set of best practices and leveraging the lessons the cloud provider will have learned from their other customers?

The United Kingdom's National Audit Office (NOA) advanced 12 pages of questions that the Board's audit committee might consider asking concerning cloud governance. Table 10.3 focuses on twenty questions using NOA's list related to strategic oversight, risk management, compliance, and other governance considerations that are particularly relevant to Board discussions about the cloud.

Table 10.3: Questions from the Audit Committee on Cloud Governance, as Adapted from the U.K. National Audit Office.[207]

Questions the Audit Committee Should Consider Concerning Cloud Governance
1. What are the priorities for the digital strategy?
2. Has the cloud strategy had input from an appropriate range of stakeholders?
3. Have key stakeholders been engaged through a comprehensive change management strategy?
4. Is there an exit strategy?
5. Has the organization addressed lock-in considerations?
6. Will there be clear accountability between the organization and the cloud provider?
7. Is there a plan for dealing with legacy technology?
8. Have cloud concentration risks been considered?
9. What extra skills and capacity will be needed?
10. What are the CSP's security accreditation and protocols?
11. Is there an understanding of what assurances are available from the CSP?
12. Where is the CSP's infrastructure physically situated, and in what jurisdiction(s) is the organization's data being held and accessed?
13. Do contracts cover data protection risks, licensing risks, and changes of jurisdiction?
14. Are technical risks covered with clear responsibilities and mitigating actions?
15. Have business continuity plans been updated?
16. Are plans in place to cover the event of data loss?

Table 10.3 (continued)

Questions the Audit Committee Should Consider Concerning Cloud Governance
17. Are financial controls fully tested and compliant with best practice?
18. Are responsibilities clear for system changes, upgrades, patches?
19. Does management scrutinize Service Organization Controls report findings?
20. Is there a regular review to ensure that the pricing model continues to be the best fit for the organization's needs?

Is the Board Asking the Right Questions about Artificial Intelligence?

Crafting appropriate questions is an integral part of the Board's due care responsibilities. Relevant and targeted questions help to facilitate meaningful discussions between the Board, management, and other stakeholders. Table 10.4 presents questions that the National Association of Corporate Directors (NACD) advanced that Board members can ask about AI governance.

Table 10.4: Questions from the Board on AI Governance, as Adapted from NACD.[208]

Questions the Board Should Consider Concerning AI Governance
1. What steps are management taking to ensure that AI governance is culturally embedded throughout the organization, rather than just a top-down policy approach?
2. How are we aligning our AI strategy with the company's broader corporate goals?
3. What is the company's approach to ensuring the quality and readiness of data for AI, and how are we addressing data gaps that could impact our AI goals?
4. How are we balancing the need for innovation with management of AI-related risks across the organization?
5. What processes do we have in place to ensure our AI governance model remains agile and resilient in the face of rapid technological and regulatory changes?
6. Who within the organization is responsible for managing and reporting to the board on the AI program and its success?
7. Has the organization delegated AI oversight to committees (drawing on board and senior leadership), outlining which aspects of AI governance should be managed by each committee?
8. Does the board currently possess sufficient AI knowledge, or is there a need for targeted training to enhance their understanding and oversight capabilities?

Board meeting agendas must include the topics of AI and the cloud to strengthen governance and organizational resilience. Harvard Law School suggests other ways management should engage the Board about AI.[209]

- Risk Management of Critical AI Uses: Provide reports to the Board about AI, their data sources, risks, and mitigation strategies.
- Incident Response: Ensure timely Board notification of significant AI incidents, response actions, and business impacts.
- Board Oversight: Include AI risks as a regular board agenda item and assign clear management responsibility for compliance.
- Focused Governance: Establish an AI committee to discuss AI compliance, report on AI enterprise risks, and obtain feedback about new AI policies.

Call to Action

1. Evaluate whether to recruit Board members with cloud and AI experience.
2. Strengthen digital literacy and fluency of the Board members.
3. Create agendas that encourage an engaging dialog about cloud and AI.
4. Present reports to the Board about cloud breaches, cloud/AI risks, and mitigation strategies.
5. Consider establishing an AI committee to focus on AI governance.

Box 10.1: Fiduciary Duties
Board of Directors and Fiduciary Duties
Board Source defines fiduciary duty as,

> Board members, as stewards of public trust, must act for the good of the organization rather than for the benefit of themselves. Fiduciary duty requires board members to be objective, responsible, honest, trustworthy, and efficient. They are expected to exercise reasonable care in all decision-making, honor their duties under the law and avoid placing the organization under unnecessary risk. It also means board members ensure the programs align with the mission and that the impact of said programs is measured and reasonable.[210]

Table 10.5 presents the Cornell Law School Legal Information Institute's perspective on the class of duties that comprise the fiduciary duties of board members.

Table 10.5: Perspectives on Fiduciary Responsibilities of US Boards, as Adapted from Cornell Law School.[212]

Fiduciary Duties	Description
Duty of Care	Directors inform themselves prior to making a business decision, of all material information reasonably available to them. Moreover, a director may not simply accept the information presented. Rather, the director must assess the information with a "critical eye," to protect the interests of the corporations and its stockholders.
Duty of Loyalty	All directors and officers of a corporation working in their capacities as corporate fiduciaries must act without personal economic conflict.
Duty of Good Faith	A corporation's directors and officers must advance interests of the corporation and fulfill their duties without violating the law.
Duty of Confidentiality	A corporation's directors and officers must keep corporate information confidential and not disclose it for their own benefit
Duty of Prudence	A trustee must administer a trust with a degree of care, skill, and caution that a prudent trustee would exercise.
Duty of Disclosure	Requires directors to act with "complete candor." In certain circumstances, this requires the directors to disclose to the stockholders "all of the facts and circumstances" relevant to the directors' decision.

Board of Directors and the Duty of Care

The *duty of care* is one of the most nuanced responsibilities of a board member, expecting informed and discerning decisions be made by board members on behalf of organizational stakeholders. These are six Duty of Care-related responsibilities of Board members, as adapted from OnBoard.[211]

1. Be Present: Attend and actively participate in board and committee meetings.
2. Be Involved: Ask questions, engage in discussions, advocate for progress, and offer ideas or solutions.
3. Be Prepared: Review board agendas and meeting materials in advance and solicit expert advice when appropriate.
4. Be Thorough: Conduct due diligence. Investigate available options and alternatives before making decisions, such as vendor selection.
5. Be Informed: Know your organization's mission, people, culture, community, budget, processes, policies, and procedures.
6. Be Alert: Pay attention to your organization's operations, how it is serving its mission, whether it has the resources it needs to effectively act on that mission, and whether it is following appropriate laws and regulations.

Is the Board prepared to govern the organization's digital transformation? Table 10.6 lists examples of questions presented by the Harvard Business Review that my help management assess the Board preparedness.

Table 10.6: Questions Management Should Ask to Assess Member Preparedness, as Adapted from HBR.[213]

Preparedness Question	Description
1. Does the board understand the implications of digital and technology well enough to provide valuable guidance?	Building up the board's digital aptitude isn't about turning directors into proficient technologists. Rather, the goal is for the board to understand the implications of technology and digital on the business and sources of revenue.
2. Is the digital transformation fundamentally changing how the business (and sector) creates value?	In the context of a digital transformation, there are three vectors of value: scale (is the new value big enough?), source (where is the value coming from?), and scope (are we thinking long term enough?).
3. How does the board know if the digital transformation is working?	Digital transformations are complex programs with dozens or even hundreds of initiatives. This can generate a soothing level of activity, but it tells you very little about whether your digital transformation is on track. To get past the noise, boards can start with a hard-nosed assessment of the strategy and road map.
4. Does the board have a sufficiently expansive view of talent?	The digital-talent discussion at the board level is often limited to expressing the need to hire more executives who are digital natives or people from consumer-facing companies that might be further along on their digital journeys. Given the scope of change required across the entire business, boards must develop an expansive view and pressure test the talent road map as much as they might the technology or digital-transformation road map.
5. Does the board have a clear view of emerging threats?	Digital expands companies' competitive footprint by blurring traditional sector boundaries. While this creates new opportunities for companies to participate in emerging ecosystems, it also generates a more complex set of threats to assess. On the risk side, boards generally have a clear understanding of the importance of cybersecurity. Many have a framework, vetted by third parties, to help evaluate cyber risk. Digital, however, opens new and different pools of risk. Regulations about privacy grab headlines, but local compliance or national security laws, for example, have introduced unforeseen risks to businesses when their servers are located in those corresponding location.

Notes

1 Berger, M. (1997, November 7). *Isaiah Berlin, Philosopher And Pluralist, Is Dead at 88*. The New York Times. https://www.nytimes.com/1997/11/07/arts/isaiah-berlin-philosopher-and-pluralist-is-dead-at-88.html

2 *Sicilian Proverbs* (n.d.). List of Proverbs. https://www.listofproverbs.com/source/s/sicilian_proverb/12.htm

3 Levitas, R. (1990). *Educated Hope: Ernst Bloch on Abstract and Concrete Utopia*. Utopian Studies, 1(2), 13–26. http://www.jstor.org/stable/20718998

4 *Chaos Definition*. (n.d.). Cambridge Dictionary. https://dictionary.cambridge.org/us/dictionary/english/chaos

5 Cecci, H. (2020, February 25). *Move From Cloud First to Cloud Smart to Improve Cloud Journey Success*. Gartner. https://www.gartner.com/en/conferences/hub/cloud-conferences/insights/cloud-smart-best-practices

6 Albert Einstein Quotes (n.d.) BrainyQuote. https://www.brainyquote.com/quotes/albert_einstein_121993

7 Camillus, J. C. (2008, May). *Strategy as a Wicked Problem*. Harvard Business Review. https://hbr.org/2008/05/strategy-as-a-wicked-problem

8 Rittel, H. W. J., & Webber, M. M. (1973). *Dilemmas in a General Theory of Planning*. Policy Sciences, 4(2), 155–169. https://doi.org/10.1007/BF01405730

9 Camillus, J. C. (2008, May). *Strategy as a Wicked Problem*. Harvard Business Review. https://hbr.org/2008/05/strategy-as-a-wicked-problem

10 Barry Commoner Quotes. (n.d.) BrainyQuote. https://www.brainyquote.com/quotes/barry_commoner_392355

11 Thuraisingham, B. (2020, October). *Cloud Governance*. In 2020 IEEE 13th International Conference on Cloud Computing. (pp. 86–90). Institute of Electrical and Electronics Engineers. https://ieeexplore.ieee.org/document/9284234

12 Baker, J. (2011). The Technological-Organization-Environment Framework. In Dwivedi, Y., Wade, M. and Schneberger, S. (Eds). *Information Systems Theory: Explaining and Predicting Our Digital Society*. Springer, New York, NY, pp. 231–246.

13 Baker, J. (2011). The Technological-Organization-Environment Framework. In Dwivedi, Y., Wade, M. and Schneberger, S. (Eds). *Information Systems Theory: Explaining and Predicting Our Digital Society*. Springer, New York, NY, pp. 231–246.

14 *The Future Depends on What You Do Today*. (n.d.). Quotespedia. https://www.quotespedia.org/authors/m/mahatma-gandhi/the-future-depends-on-what-you-do-today-mahatma-gandhi/

15 *2025 Future of Jobs Report*. (2025, January 7). World Economic Forum. https://www.weforum.org/publications/the-future-of-jobs-report-2025/digest/

16 *What is Quantum Computing?* (2024, April 5). McKinsey & Company. https://www.mckinsey.com/featured-insights/mckinsey-explainers/what-is-quantum-computing

17 Alsop, T. (2024, November 18). *Quantum Technology Market Revenue Worldwide* 2040. https://www.statista.com/statistics/1317754/global-quantum-technology-market-revenue-forecast/

18 *Quantum Computing Market Size, Share & Trends Analysis*. (2025, March 3). Fortune Business Insights. https://www.fortunebusinessinsights.com/quantum-computing-market-104855

19 *Quantum Technology Monitor*. (April 2024). McKinsey Digital. https://www.mckinsey.com/~/media/mckinsey/business%20functions/mckinsey%20digital/our%20insights/steady%20progress%20in%20approaching%20the%20quantum%20advantage/quantum-technology-monitor-april-2024.pdf

20 *State of Quantum Computing: Building a Quantum Economy*. (2022, September). World Economic Forum. https://www3.weforum.org/docs/WEF_State_of_Quantum_Computing_2022.pdf

21 IBM Cloud Education. (2021, September 16). *What is Artificial Intelligence?* IBM. https://www.ibm.com/cloud/learn/what-is-artificial-intelligence?lnk=hpmls_buwi

22 Linthicum, D. (2024, October 7). *Agentic AI Fundamentals: Architectures, Frameworks, and Applications* [Video]. LinkedIn. https://www.linkedin.com/learning/agentic-ai-fundamentals-architectures-frameworks-and-applications

23 Vailsheri, L.S. (2025, January 24). *Global Market Value of Agentic AI in 2024 & 2030*. https://www.statista.com/statistics/1552183/global-agentic-ai-market-value/

24 Marr, B. (2024, September 16). *Agentic AI: The Next Big Breakthrough That's Transforming Business and Technology*. Bernard Marr & Co. https://bernardmarr.com/agentic-ai-the-next-big-breakthrough-thats-transforming-business-and-technology/

25 Linthicum, D. (2024, November 13). *Leveraging AI Agents in Cloud Computing* [Video]. LinkedIn. https://www.linkedin.com/learning/leveraging-ai-agents-in-cloud-computing

26 Linthicum, D. (2025, April 6). *Agentic AI and the ROI Disconnect: Why Enterprises Must Take a Measured Approach*. LinkedIn. https://www.linkedin.com/pulse/agentic-ai-roi-disconnect-why-enterprises-must-take-david-linthicum-gr9ee/

27 Clement, J. (2025, March 11). *Global Cloud Gaming Market Revenue Worldwide 2017 to 2029*. Statista. https://www.statista.com/forecasts/1390137/cloud-gaming-market-global

28 *What is the IoT?* (n.d.) IBM. https://www.ibm.com/think/topics/internet-of-things

29 Vailshery, L.S. (2024, September 11). *IoT Connections Worldwide 2022–2033*. Statista. https://www.statista.com/statistics/1183457/iot-connected-devices-worldwide/

30 *The Internet of Things: Market Data and Analysis*. (2024, June). Statista. https://www.statista.com/study/109197/internet-of-things-market-outlook-report/

31 Taylor, P. A*mount of Data Created, Consumed, and Stored 2010–2023, with Forecasts to 2028*. (2024, November 21). Statista. https://www.statista.com/statistics/871513/worldwide-data-created/

32 Bartley, K. (2024, December 11). *Big Data Statistics: How Much Data is there in the World?* Rivery. https://rivery.io/blog/big-data-statistics-how-much-data-is-there-in-the-world/

33 DNA Data Storage Alliance. (n.d.) https://dnastoragealliance.org/

34 Raza, S. (2024, February). *DNA as Data Storage*. University of Cambridge and PHG Foundation. https://www.phgfoundation.org/wp-content/uploads/2024/02/DNA-as-data-storage.pdf

35 Friedman, T., & Judah, S. (2016, June 30). *Data Risks in the Internet of Things Demand Extensive Information Governance*. Gartner. https://www.gartner.com/en/documents/3362117/data-risks-in-the-internet-of-things-demand-extensive-in

36 *What is Edge Computing?* (2021, March 31). RedHat. https://www.redhat.com/en/topics/edge-computing/what-is-edge-computing

37 Blanton, N. (2021, November 10). *What is the Future of Wearable Technology in Healthcare?* Baylor College of Medicine. https://blogs.bcm.edu/2021/11/10/what-is-the-future-of-wearable-technology-in-healthcare/

38 U.S. GAO. (2012, September 27). *Medical Devices: FDA Should Expand Its Consideration of Information Security for Certain Types of Devices*. https://www.gao.gov/products/gao-12-816

39 McLuhan, M. (n.d.). *A Quote from Marshall McLuhan*. GoodReads. https://www.goodreads.com/quotes/350791-we-become-what-we-behold-we-shape-our-tools-and

40 National Institute of Standards and Technology Computer Security Resource Center. (n.d.). *Cyber-Attack – Glossary*. NIST. https://csrc.nist.gov/glossary/term/cyber_attack

41 National Institute of Standards and Technology Computer Security Resource Center. (n.d.). *Breach – Glossary*. NIST. https://csrc.nist.gov/glossary/term/breach

42 *Cost of a Data Breach Report 2024.* (2024, July 30). IBM. https://www.ibm.com/reports/data-breach

43 Lewis, T. (2024, July 18). *Ticketmaster breach highlights consequences of cybercrime-as-a-service marketplaces and shared responsibility model.* Security Information Watch. https://www.securityinfowatch.com/cybersecurity/article/55126907/ticketmaster-breach-highlights-consequences-of-cybercrime-as-a-service-marketplaces-and-shared-responsibility-model

44 Oladimeji, S., & Kerner, S. M. (2023, November 3). *SolarWinds Hack Explained: Everything You Need to Know.* TechTarget. https://www.techtarget.com/whatis/feature/SolarWinds-hack-explained-Everything-you-need-to-know

45 *Supply Chain Attacks.* (2022, April 5). Microsoft. https://docs.microsoft.com/en-us/microsoft-365/security/intelligence/supply-chain-malware?view=o365-worldwide

46 McGee, M. K. (2020, September 11). *Tally of Those Affected by Blackbaud Hack Soars.* BankInfoSecurity. https://www.bankinfosecurity.com/blackbaud-chart-update-a-14982

47 U.S. Cybersecurity & Infrastructure Security Agency. (n.d.). *Stop Ransomware.* CISA.Gov. https://www.cisa.gov/stopransomware

48 *Cost of a Data Breach Report 2024.* (2024, July 30). IBM. https://www.ibm.com/reports/data-breach

49 *AI to Drive 165% Increase in Data Center Power Demand by 2030.* (2025, February 4). Goldman Sachs. https://www.goldmansachs.com/insights/articles/ai-to-drive-165-increase-in-data-center-power-demand-by-2030

50 *Google Environmental Report 2024.* (2024, July). Google. https://www.gstatic.com/gumdrop/sustainability/google-2024-environmental-report.pdf

51 Li, P. Yang, P., Islam, M., Ren, R. (2025, January 15). *Making AI Less "Thirsty": Uncovering and Addressing the Secret Water Footprint of AI Models.* University of California, Riverside. https://arxiv.org/pdf/2304.03271

52 *Electricity 2024 Report.* (2024, January). International Energy Agency. https://www.iea.org/news/clean-sources-of-generation-are-set-to-cover-all-of-the-world-s-additional-electricity-demand-over-the-next-three-years

53 Vincent. M. (2025, February 5). *How AI's Transformative Impact on Data Centers Is Driving Unprecedented Industry Growth, Innovation, and Global Expansion.* Data Center Frontier. https://www.datacenterfrontier.com/machine-learning/article/55265866/how-ais-transformative-impact-on-data-centers-is-driving-unprecedented-industry-growth-innovation-and-global-expansion

54 McGeady, C. Majkut, J. Harithas, B. and Smith, K. (2025, March 3). *The Electricity Supply Bottleneck on U.S. AI Dominance.* Center for Strategic and International Studies. https://www.csis.org/analysis/electricity-supply-bottleneck-us-ai-dominance

55 Starcloud (n.d.) https://www.starcloud.com/

56 *Axiom In Space Goes All-in on AWS for its Enterprise Cloud Service Needs Here on Earth.* (2023, November 27). https://www.axiomspace.com/release/amazon-web-services-all-in

57 *EU Directive 2023/1791 on Energy Efficiency.* (2023, September 20). European Parliament. https://eur-lex.europa.eu/eli/dir/2023/1791/oj

58 Watson, E. *Fast Fashion.* (n.d.). Fast Fashion. https://www.cleanup.org.au/fastfashion

59 *Special Publication 800–145: The NIST Definition of Cloud Computing.* (No. 800–145). (2011, September). NIST. https://csrc.nist.gov/publications/detail/sp/800-145/final

60 European Union Agency for Cybersecurity. (2009, November 20). *Cloud Computing Risk Assessment.* ENISA. https://www.enisa.europa.eu/publications/cloud-computing-risk-assessment

61 Badger, L., Bohn, R. Leaf, D. Liu, F., Mao, J., Messina, J., & Tong, J. (2011, September). *Special Publication 500–292: Cloud Computing Reference Architecture.* NIST. https://tsapps.nist.gov/publication/get_pdf.cfm?pub_id=909505

62 Stryker, C. and Kavlakoglu, E. (2024, August 16). IBM. *What is Artificial Intelligence?* https://www.ibm.com/topics/artificial-intelligence

63 Badger, L., Bohn, R. Leaf, D. Liu, F., Mao, J., Messina, J., & Tong, J. (2011, September). *Special Publication 500–292: Cloud Computing Reference Architecture.* NIST. https://tsapps.nist.gov/publication/get_pdf.cfm?pub_id=909505

64 Badger, L., Bohn, R. Leaf, D. Liu, F., Mao, J., Messina, J., & Tong, J. (2011, September). *Special Publication 500–292: Cloud Computing Reference Architecture.* NIST. https://tsapps.nist.gov/publication/get_pdf.cfm?pub_id=909505

65 *What is Cloud Computing?* (2024, July 31). McKinsey & Company. https://www.mckinsey.com/featured-insights/mckinsey-explainers/what-is-cloud-computing

66 Erickson, J. (2024, June 21). *The Role and Benefits of AI in Cloud Computing.* Oracle. https://www.oracle.com/artificial-intelligence/ai-cloud-computing/

67 Grance, T., Mell, P. (2011, September). *Special Publication 800–145, The NIST Definition of Cloud Computing.* National Institute of Standards and Technology. https://csrc.nist.gov/publications/detail/sp/800-145/final

68 Badger, L., Bohn, R. Leaf, D. Liu, F., Mao, J., Messina, J., & Tong, J. (2011, September). *Special Publication 500–292: Cloud Computing Reference Architecture.* NIST. https://tsapps.nist.gov/publication/get_pdf.cfm?pub_id=909505

69 Linthicum, D. (2021, April 2). *Are Industry Clouds an Opportunity or a Distraction?* InfoWorld. https://www.infoworld.com/article/3613714/are-industry-clouds-an-opportunity-or-a-distraction.html

70 *What is Sovereign Cloud?* (2024 May 8). IBM. https://www.ibm.com/topics/sovereign-cloud

71 Tozzi, C. (2024, September 4). *Microclouds: The Next Big Thing in Cloud Computing or Just Another Edge Strategy?* ITPro Today. https://www.itprotoday.com/cloud-computing/microclouds-the-next-big-thing-in-cloud-computing-or-just-another-edge-strategy-

72 Linthicum, D. (2024, May 11). LinkedIn. *The Rise of "Micro-Clouds": How Smaller Providers Are Challenging the Big Three.* https://www.linkedin.com/pulse/rise-micro-clouds-how-smaller-providers-challenging-big-linthicum-gly1e

73 *Definition of Managed Security Service Provider – Gartner Information Technology Glossary.* (n.d.). Gartner. https://www.gartner.com/en/information-technology/glossary/mssp-managed-security-service-provider

74 Manral, V. (2023, July 28). *Generative AI: Proposed Shared Responsibility Model.* Cloud Security Alliance. https://cloudsecurityalliance.org/blog/2023/07/28/generative-ai-proposed-shared-responsibility-model

75 *8 Criteria to Ensure you Select the Right Cloud Service Provider.* (n.d.). Cloud Industry Forum. https://www.cloudindustryforum.org/content/8-criteria-ensure-you-select-right-cloud-service-provider

76 Witkowski, W. (2021, October 5). *Facebook Outage, by the Numbers: Largest Outage Ever Tracked Could Cost Millions.* MarketWatch. https://www.marketwatch.com/story/facebook-outage-by-the-numbers-largest-outage-ever-tracked-could-cost-millions-11633387093

77 Bigelow, S. (2023, December). *Cloud Sprawl.* TechTarget. https://searchcloudcomputing.techtarget.com/definition/cloud-sprawl

78 Linthicum, D. (2019, July 16). *How to Deal with Cloud Complexity.* InfoWorld. https://www.infoworld.com/article/2262010/how-to-deal-with-cloud-complexity.html

79 Bigelow, S. J. (2024, February 8). *How to build a Cloud Center of Excellence in 9 Steps.* TechTarget. https://searchcloudcomputing.techtarget.com/tip/How-to-build-a-cloud-center-of-excellence

80 Holmes, O. W. (n.d.). *A Quote by Oliver Wendell Holmes Jr.* GoodReads. https://www.goodreads.com/quotes/7613719-greatness-is-not-in-where-we-stand-but-in-what

81 Marr, B. (2024, November 18). *The 7 Revolutionary Cloud Computing Trends That Will Define Business Success in 2025*. https://bernardmarr.com/the-7-revolutionary-cloud-computing-trends-that-will-define-business-success-in-2025/

82 *The Cloud Strategy Cookbook*. (2021, February 17). Gartner. https://www.gartner.com/smarter withgartner/the-cloud-strategy-cookbook

83 Awasthi, R. (2023, February 13). *Cloud First to Cloud Smart: A Strategic Shift*. Cloud Security Alliance. https://cloudsecurityalliance.org/blog/2023/02/13/cloud-first-to-cloud-smart-a-strategic-shift

84 *Definition of Cloud Strategy – Gartner Information Technology Glossary*. (n.d.). Gartner. https://www.gartner.com/en/information-technology/glossary/cloud-strategy

85 *The Cloud Strategy Cookbook*. (2021, February 17). Gartner. https://www.gartner.com/smarter withgartner/the-cloud-strategy-cookbook

86 Bigelow, S. J. (2024, February 23). *How to build a Cloud Center of Excellence in 9 Steps*. TechTarget. https://searchcloudcomputing.techtarget.com/tip/How-to-build-a-cloud-center-of-excellence

87 *Cloud Computing Study 2024*. (2024, August 27). Foundry. https://foundryco.com/research/cloud-computing/

88 *2024 State of the Cloud Report*. (2024, March 12). Flexera. https://www.flexera.com/about-us/press-center/flexera-2024-state-of-the-cloud-managing-spending-top-challenge

89 Ashwood, P. (2023, August 31). *The Common Cloud Misconfigurations That Lead to Cloud Data Breaches*. Crowdstrike. https://www.crowdstrike.com/en-us/blog/common-cloud-security-misconfigurations/

90 *Key Practices of the Capability Maturity Model Version 1.1*. (1993, February). Carnegie Mellon University Software Engineering Institute. https://insights.sei.cmu.edu/documents/1093/1993_005_001_16214.pdf

91 Paulk, M., Curtis, W., Chrissis, M.B., & Weber, C. (1993). *Capability Maturity Model for Software (Version 1.1)*. Carnegie Mellon University, Software Engineering Institute. (CMU/SEI-93-TR-024). https://resources.sei.cmu.edu/asset_files/technicalreport/1993_005_001_16211.pdf

92 *Cloud Maturity Model Rev. 4*. (n.d.). Open Alliance for Cloud Adoption. https://oaca-project.org/cmm/

93 Marston, S., Li, Z., Bandyopadhyay, S., Zhang, J. and Ghalsasi, A. (2011, April) *Cloud Computing – The Business Perspective*. Decision Supports Systems. https://www.sciencedirect.com/science/article/abs/pii/S0167923610000293?via%3Dihub

94 Efrati, A. and McLaughlin, K. (2019, February 25). *As AWS Use Soars, Companies Surprised by Cloud Bills*. The Information. https://www.theinformation.com/articles/as-aws-use-soars-companies-surprised-by-cloud-bills

95 *2024 State of the Cloud Report*. (2024, March 12). Flexera. https://www.flexera.com/about-us/press-center/flexera-2024-state-of-the-cloud-managing-spending-top-challenge

96 *How to Manage and Optimize Costs of Public Cloud IaaS and PaaS*. (23 March 2020). Gartner. https://www.gartner.com/en/documents/3982411/how-to-manage-and-optimize-costs-of-public-cloud-iaas-an

97 *What is Cloud ROI?* (n.d.). VMware. https://www.vmware.com/topics/glossary/content/cloud-roi.html

98 *What is Cloud Computing?* (2024, July 31). McKinsey. https://www.mckinsey.com/featured-insights/mckinsey-explainers/what-is-cloud-computing

99 *Good Practice Guide: Guidance for Audit Committees on Cloud Services*. (2024, September). United Kingdom National Audit Office. https://www.nao.org.uk/wp-content/uploads/2021/04/guidance-for-audit-committees-on-cloud-services-2024.pdf

100 Sutton, D. (2017, October 12). *20 Transformational Quotes on Change Management*. TopRight Partners. https://www.toprightpartners.com/insights/20-transformational-quotes-on-change-management/

101 Harvard Business School Online's Business Insights Blog. (2020, March 20). *Types of Organizational Change & How to Manage Them*. Harvard Business School. https://online.hbs.edu/blog/post/types-of-organizational-change

102 Lucid Content Team. (n.d.). *All About Cloud Change Management*. Lucidchart. https://www.lucidchart.com/blog/cloud-change-management

103 *What is cloud management?* (2018, March 7). Red Hat. https://www.redhat.com/en/topics/cloud-computing/what-is-cloud-management

104 Protiviti & North Carolina State University. (2025, February 11). *Executive Perspectives on Top Risks*. Protiviti. https://erm.ncsu.edu/wp-content/uploads/sites/41/2025/02/nc-state-protiviti-2025-top-risks-survey-final-250213.pdf

105 Lucid Content Team. (n.d.). *All About Cloud Change Management*. Lucidchart. https://www.lucidchart.com/blog/cloud-change-management

106 *What is Change Management?* (n.d.). American Society for Quality. https://asq.org/quality-resources/change-management

107 Gianni, J. (2021, June 9). *Change Management: 6 Reasons it Fails*. The Enterprisers Project. https://enterprisersproject.com/article/2021/6/change-management-6-reasons-fails

108 Jones, R., Kamen, M., & Kearns-Manolatos, D. (2021, October 21). *Cloud Enabled Workforce*. Deloitte. https://www2.deloitte.com/us/en/blog/deloitte-on-cloud-blog/2021/putting-the-power-of-a-cloud-enabled-workforce-to-work.html

109 Boleman, J., Lakshminarayanan, M., Panagakis, M., Schalk, K., Schenkewitz, L., & Van Order, B. (2018, May). *Best Practices for Developing and Growing a Cloud-Enabled Workforce*. Cloud Standards Customer Council. https://www.omg.org/cloud/deliverables/CSCC-Best-Practices-for-Developing-and-Growing-a-Cloud-Enabled-Workforce.pdf

110 *Learning and Development: A Comprehensive Guide*. (n.d.). Academy to Innovate HR. https://www.aihr.com/blog/learning-and-development/

111 Brassey, J., Christensen, L., & van Dam, N. (2019, February 13). *The Essential Components of a Successful L&D Strategy*. McKinsey & Company. https://www.mckinsey.com/business-functions/people-and-organizational-performance/our-insights/the-essential-components-of-a-successful-l-and-d-strategy

112 Arcitura. (n.d.). https://www.arcitura.com/

113 Linthicum, D. (n.d.). *Cloud Computing Insider*. https://davidlinthicum.com/resources

114 Rose, E. (2024, May 21). *How AR Onboarding Can Transform Training Programs*. https://builtbyrose.co/how-ar-onboarding-can-transform-training-programs/

115 Dogan, C. (2018). *From the Basement to the Cloud | The Role of the CIO over Four Decades*. Deloitte. https://www2.deloitte.com/content/dam/Deloitte/ar/Documents/technology/THE-ROLE-OF-THE-CIO-OVERF-OUR-DECADES.pdf

116 Kark, K., Nann, E., Nguyen Phillips, A., & Perton, M. (2020, April 10). *The New CIO: Business-Savvy Technologist*. Deloitte. https://www2.deloitte.com/us/en/insights/focus/cio-insider-business-insights/the-new-cio.html

117 Churchill, W. (1993). *The Price of Greatness*. International Churchill Society. https://winstonchurchill.org/old-site/learn/speeches-learn/the-price-of-greatness/

118 Kinsella, D. (2019, January 15). *Extended Enterprise Risk Management to be a Focus in 2019*. Deloitte. https://www2.deloitte.com/us/en/pages/about-deloitte/articles/press-releases/deloitte-poll-extended-enterprise-risk-management-to-be-2019-focus.html

119 Manral, V. (2023, July 28). *Generative AI: Proposed Shared Responsibility Model*. Cloud Security Alliance. https://cloudsecurityalliance.org/blog/2023/07/28/generative-ai-proposed-shared-responsibility-model

120 Campitelli, V., Mezzio, S., & Stein, M. (2020, July 12). *Managing the Impact of Cloud Computing*. The CPA Journal. https://www.cpajournal.com/2020/07/13/managing-the-impact-of-cloud-computing/

121 Cloud Passage. (2020, August 26). *Shared Responsibility Model Explained*. Cloud Security Alliance. https://cloudsecurityalliance.org/blog/2020/08/26/shared-responsibility-model-explained/

122 Deloitte. (2019). *Cloud Computing Risk Intelligence Map*. https://www2.deloitte.com/content/dam/Deloitte/in/Documents/risk/in-ra-roap-map-noexp.pdf

123 McLean, M. (2024, November 4). Embroker. *5 cyber insurance claims: Real-world examples every business should know*. https://www.embroker.com/blog/cyber-insurance-claims-examples/

124 Schandl, A., & Foster, P. L. (2019, January). *COSO Internal Control – Integrated Framework: An Implementation Guide for the Healthcare Provider Industry*. Committee of Sponsoring Organizations of the Treadway Commission. https://www.coso.org/documents/coso-crowe-coso-internal-control-integrated-framework.pdf

125 Cloud Controls Matrix Working Group. (2021, December). *Cloud Controls Matrix (Version 4)*. Cloud Security Alliance. https://cloudsecurityalliance.org/research/cloud-controls-matrix/

126 Moorcraft, B. (2020, October 26). *A Risk Manager's Rise to the C-Suite and the Boardroom*. Insurance Business Magazine. https://www.insurancebusinessmag.com/us/risk-management/news/a-risk-managers-rise-to-the-csuite-and-the-boardroom-237239.aspx

127 European Network and Information Security Agency. (2006, June). *Risk Management – Principles and Inventories for Risk Management*. ENISA. https://www.enisa.europa.eu/publications/risk-management-principles-and-inventories-for-risk-management-risk-assessment-methods-and-tools

128 Piney, C. (2003). *Risk Identification: Combining the Tools to Deliver the Goods*. Paper presented at PMI® Global Congress 2003 – EMEA, The Hague, South Holland, The Netherlands. Newtown Square, PA: Project Management Institute.

129 Deloitte. (2019, April 15). *Scenario Planning and Wargaming for the Risk Management Toolkit*. WSJ. https://deloitte.wsj.com/articles/scenario-planning-and-wargaming-for-the-risk-management-toolkit-01555376533

130 Forrest, W., Li, S., Tamburro, I., & Van Kuiken, S. (2021, April 30). *Four Ways Boards Can Shape the Cloud Agenda*. McKinsey & Company. https://www.mckinsey.com/business-functions/mckinsey-digital/our-insights/four-ways-boards-can-shape-the-cloud-agenda

131 Cloud Controls Matrix Working Group. (2021, December). *Cloud Controls Matrix (Version 4)*. Cloud Security Alliance. https://cloudsecurityalliance.org/research/cloud-controls-matrix/

132 Diffie, W. (n.d.). Quotemaster. https://www.quotemaster.org/q39d0d\450f73c57e5af97fc80771 68135

133 National Institute of Standards and Technology Computer Security Resource Center. (n.d.). *Cybersecurity – Glossary*. NIST. https://csrc.nist.gov/glossary/term/cybersecurity

134 Brook, C. (2020, September 29). *What is COBIT?* Digital Guardian. https://digitalguardian.com/blog/what-cobit

135 *ISO/IEC 27001 – Information security management*. (2021, February 16). International Standards Organization. https://www.iso.org/isoiec-27001-information-security.html

136 *IT Infrastructure Library*. (2022, September 27). National Health Service England. https://digital.nhs.uk/cyber-and-data-security/guidance-and-assurance/data-security-and-protection-toolkit-assessment-guides/guide-9 – it-protection/itil

137 *Cloud Security Guide for SMEs.* (2015, April 10). European Union Agency for Cybersecurity. https://www.enisa.europa.eu/publications/cloud-security-guide-for-smes

138 Joint Task Force Interagency Working Group. (2020, September). *Special Publication: Security and Privacy Controls for Information Systems and Organizations.* (No. 800–53, Revision 5). NIST. https://nvlpubs.nist.gov/nistpubs/SpecialPublications/NIST.SP.800-53r5.pdf

139 *Framework for Improving Critical Infrastructure Cybersecurity.* (2018, April 16). NIST https://nvlpubs.nist.gov/nistpubs/CSWP/NIST.CSWP.04162018.pdf

140 *Critical Security Controls Version 8.* (2021, May 18). Center for Internet Security. https://www.cisecurity.org/controls/v8/

141 *HITRUST Alliance Common Security Framework: Information Risk Management.* (2021, October 20). HITRUST Alliance. https://hitrustalliance.net/product-tool/hitrust-csf/

142 Cloud Controls Matrix Working Group. (2021, December 8). *Cloud Controls Matrix (Version 4).* Cloud Security Alliance. https://cloudsecurityalliance.org/research/cloud-controls-matrix/

143 *Framework for Improving Critical Infrastructure Cybersecurity.* (2018, April 16). NIST https://nvlpubs.nist.gov/nistpubs/CSWP/NIST.CSWP.04162018.pdf

144 *What is Cloud Security? Cloud Security Defined.* (n.d.). IBM. https://www.ibm.com/topics/cloud-security

145 *Security Guidance for Critical Areas of Focus in Cloud Computing.* (2017, July 26.). Cloud Security Alliance. https://cloudsecurityalliance.org/artifacts/security-guidance-v4/

146 Greis, J., Sorel, M. *The Cybersecurity Provider's Next Opportunity: Making AI Safer.* (2024, November 14). McKinsey. https://www.mckinsey.com/capabilities/risk-and-resilience/our-insights/the-cybersecurity-providers-next-opportunity-making-ai-safer

147 *Cloud Incident Response Framework* (2021, May 4), Cloud Security Alliance. https://cloudsecurityalliance.org/research/topics/cloud-incident-response

148 *Cloud Incident Response Framework* (2021, May 4), Cloud Security Alliance. https://cloudsecurityalliance.org/research/topics/cloud-incident-response

149 *Cloud Incident Response Framework* (2021, May 4), Cloud Security Alliance. https://cloudsecurityalliance.org/research/topics/cloud-incident-response

150 *Cloud Incident Response Framework* (2021, May 4), Cloud Security Alliance. https://cloudsecurityalliance.org/research/topics/cloud-incident-response

151 Borchert, O., Connelly, S. Mitchell, S. & Rose, S. (2020, August). *Special Publication 800–207: Zero Trust Architecture.* NIST. https://doi.org/10.6028/NIST.SP.800-207

152 *Benefits & Challenges of Zero Trust Security.* (n.d.) NordLayer. https://nordlayer.com/learn/zero-trust/benefits/#what-are-the-main-benefits-of-zero-trust-security

153 *Altaba, Formerly Known as Yahoo!, Charged With Failing to Disclose Massive Cybersecurity Breach; Agrees To Pay $35 Million.* (2018, April 24). U.S. Securities and Exchange Commission. https://www.sec.gov/news/press-release/2018-71

154 *Yahoo Cuts Sale Price to Verizon by $350 Million After Hacks* (2017, February 21). NBC News. https://www.nbcnews.com/business/business-news/yahoo-cuts-sale-price-verizon-350-million-after-hacks-n723546

155 *Yahoo! Inc. Customer Data Breach Litigation Settlement.* (n.d.). U.S. District Court Northern District of California. https://yahoodatabreachsettlement.com

156 *Security Guidance for Critical Areas of Focus in Cloud Computing.* (2017, July 26.). Cloud Security Alliance. https://cloudsecurityalliance.org/artifacts/security-guidance-v4/

157 Wadsworth Longfellow, H. (n.d.). PassItOn. https://www.passiton.com/inspirational-quotes/3760-it-takes-less-time-to-do-things-right-than-to

158 Society of Corporate Compliance and Ethics (n.d.). *Definition of Compliance.* https://www.cor poratecompliance.org/publications/compliance-dictionary

159 Edmundson, C. (2023, July 27). SANS Institute. *What is Cloud Security Compliance?* https://www.sans.org/blog/what-is-cloud-security-compliance/

160 Microsoft. (n.d.). *Navigating your Way to the Cloud: Region and Country-specific Information for Legal and Compliance Professionals.* https://www.microsoft.com/en-us/trust-center/compli ance/regional-country-compliance

161 Statista. (2024, November 12), *Fines Issued for GDPR Violations, As of September 2024, by Type of Violation.* https://www.statista.com/statistics/1172494/gdpr-fines-by-type-violation

162 Gurinaviciute, J. (2024, July 2). *Lessons To Take Away From E4.5 Billion in GDPR Fines.* Forbes. https://www.forbes.com/councils/forbestechcouncil/2024/07/02/lessons-to-take-away-from-45-billion-in-gdpr-fines/

163 *Levels of Compliance.* (n.d.) EU Cloud of Conduct. https://eucoc.cloud/en/public-register/levels-of-compliance

164 *Best Practices for Multi-Cloud Governance and Compliance.* (2024, December 19). Tata Communications. https://www.tatacommunications.com/knowledge-base/best-practices-for-multi-cloud-governance-and-compliance/

165 *General Data Protection Regulation.* (2016). https://gdpr-info.eu/

166 Regulation (EU) 2024/1689 of the European Parliament and of the Council. (2024, July 7). *AI Act.* http://data.europa.eu/eli/reg/2024/1689/oj

167 *General Data Protection Regulation.* (2016). https://gdpr-info.eu/

168 Organisation for Economic Co-Operation and Development. (2013, November 28). *Anti-Corruption Ethics and Compliance Handbook for Business.* https://www.oecd.org/corruption/anti-corruption-ethics-and-compliance-handbook-for-business.htm

169 Government of Canada. (2015, June 23). *Personal Information Protection and Electronic Documents Act.* https://laws-lois.justice.gc.ca/eng/acts/P-8.6/page-1.html

170 U.S. Congress. (1996, August 21). *Health Insurance Portability and Accountability Act.* https://www.govinfo.gov/content/pkg/PLAW-104publ191/pdf/PLAW-104publ191.pdf

171 Payment Card Industry (PCI) Security Standards Council. (2018, May). *PCI Data Security Standard.* https://www.pcisecuritystandards.org/documents/PCI_DSS_v3-2-1.pdf?agreement=true&time=1631301601091

172 U.S. Congress. (2002, July 30). *Sarbanes-Oxley Act of 2002.* https://www.congress.gov/107/plaws/publ204/PLAW-107publ204.pdf

173 U.S. Congress. (1999, November 12). *Gramm-Leach-Bliley Act.* https://www.govinfo.gov/con tent/pkg/PLAW-106publ102/pdf/PLAW-106publ102.pdf

174 U.S. Congress. (2018, December 18). *Federal Information Security and Management Act.* https://www.govinfo.gov/content/pkg/PLAW-113publ283/pdf/PLAW-113publ283.pdf

175 U.S. Department of Justice, Criminal Division (2020, June). *Evaluation of Corporate Compliance Programs* https://www.justice.gov/criminal-fraud/page/file/937501/download

176 *NASDAQ Stock Market LLC Rules, Section 5600: Corporate Governance Requirements, Part 5610: Code of Conduct.* (2009, March 12). NASDAQ. https://listingcenter.nasdaq.com/rulebook/nas daq/rules/nasdaq-5600-series

177 *NYSE Listed Corporate Manual Section 303.* (n.d). New York Stock Exchange. https://nyse guide.srorules.com/listed-company-manual/09013e2c8503fca9

178 *AI Risk Management Framework (AI RMF 1.0).* (2023, January). NIST. https://doi.org/10.6028/NIST.AI.100-1

179 *National Artificial Intelligence Initiative Act* (2021, January 1). U.S. Public Law 116-283. https://www.congress.gov/116/plaws/publ283/PLAW-116publ283.pdf

180 *AI RMF Playbook.* (2023, March 30). NIST. https://airc.nist.gov/AI_RMF_Knowledge_Base/Playbook

181 *AI Risk Management Framework: Generative AI Profile.* (2024, July). NIST Trustworthy and Responsible AI NIST AI 600-1. https://nvlpubs.nist.gov/nistpubs/ai/NIST.AI.600-1.pdf

182 *The AI Index Report 2025.* (2025, April 7). Stanford University Human-Centered Artificial Intelligence. https://aiindex.stanford.edu/report/

183 Kenton, W. (2022, July 9). *Compliance Program: Definition, Purpose, and How to Create One.* Investopedia. https://www.investopedia.com/terms/c/compliance-program.asp

184 *2024 Guidelines Manual, Chapter Eight – Sentencing of Organizations, Part B – Remedying Harm from Criminal Conduct, And Effective Compliance and Ethics Program.* (2024, November 1). United States Sentencing Commission. https://www.ussc.gov/guidelines/2024-guidelines-manual/annotated-2024-chapter-8#8b21

185 Gartner Research. (n.d.). *Define Cloud Access Security Broker.* https://www.gartner.com/en/information-technology/glossary/cloud-access-security-brokers-casbs

186 Press, D. (2018, July 16). *What is a CASB?* Cloud Security Alliance. https://cloudsecurityalliance.org/blog/2018/07/16/what-is-a-casb/

187 Bill Gates Quotes. (n.d.). BrainyQuote.com. https://www.brainyquote.com/quotes/bill_gates_626252

188 *Demystifying AI: Internal Audit Use Cases for Applying New Technology.* (2024). Auditboard and Internal Audit Foundation. https://www.theiia.org/globalassets/site/content/research/foundation/2024/demystifying_ai_2024.pdf

189 KPMG. (n.d.). *Transforming Internal Audits Through the Power of AI.* https://kpmg.com/us/en/articles/2024/transforming-internal-audits-power.html

190 AICPA. (n.d.). *System and Organization Controls: SOC Suite of Services.* https://us.aicpa.org/interestareas/frc/assuranceadvisoryservices/sorhome

191 *ISO 42001 – AI Management Systems.* (2023, December). ISO. https://www.iso.org/standard/81230.html

192 Hughes, J. *Achieving SOC 2 Compliance for AI Platforms.* (2024, September 4). Compass IT Compliance. https://www.compassitc.com/blog/achieving-soc-2-compliance-for-artificial-intelligence-ai-platforms

193 *Cloud Computing Information Assurance Framework.* (2009, November 20). ENISA. https://www.enisa.europa.eu/publications/cloud-computing-information-assurance-framework

194 *Risk Assessment.* (2009). ENISA. https://www.enisa.europa.eu/topics/cloud-and-big-data/cloud-security/risk-assessment

195 *Security and Resilience in Governmental Clouds.* (2011, January 17). ENISA. https://www.enisa.europa.eu/publications/security-and-resilience-in-governmental-clouds

196 *Survey and analysis of security parameters in cloud SLAs across the European public sector.* (2011, December 21). ENISA. https://www.enisa.europa.eu/publications/survey-and-analysis-of-security-parameters-in-cloud-slas-across-the-european-public-sector

197 *Multilayer Framework for Good Cybersecurity Practices for AI.* (2023, June 7). ENISA. https://www.enisa.europa.eu/publications/multilayer-framework-for-good-cybersecurity-practices-for-ai

198 *On-Premise vs. Cloud Auditing.* (2021, September 23). ISACA. https://www.isaca.org/resources/infographics/on-premise-vs-cloud-auditing

199 *Cloud Computing Management Audit Program.* (2010). ISACA. https://store.isaca.org/s/store#/store/browse/detail/a2S4w000004KoH1EAK

200 *COBIT Framework: Control Objectives for Information Technologies.* (2019). ISACA. https://www.isaca.org/resources/cobit

201 Van Kuiken, S. (2021, November 18). *Boards and the Cloud.* McKinsey & Company. https://www.mckinsey.com/business-functions/strategy-and-corporate-finance/our-insights/boards-and-the-cloud

202 Forrest, W., Li, S., Tamburro, I., & van Kuiken, S. (2021, April 30). *Four Ways Boards Can Shape the Cloud Agenda.* McKinsey & Company. https://www.mckinsey.com/business-functions/mckinsey-digital/our-insights/four-ways-boards-can-shape-the-cloud-agenda

203 Oxford University Press. (n.d.). *Fit for Purpose.* Lexico. https://www.lexico.com/definition/fit_for_purpose

204 PwC & The Conference Board. (2023, May 18). *Board Effectiveness: A Survey of the C-Suite.* PwC. https://www.pwc.com/us/en/services/governance-insights-center/library/board-effectiveness-and-performance-improvement.html

205 Abrash, L., Probst, A., Edelman, K. (2024, October 7). *Governance of AI: A Critical Imperative for Today's Boards.* Deloitte. https://www2.deloitte.com/us/en/insights/topics/leadership/successful-ai-oversight-may-require-more-engagement-in-the-boardroom.html

206 Venables, P., & Godfrey, N. (2022, January 13). *10 Questions to Help Boards Safely Maximize Cloud Opportunities.* Google Cloud Blog. https://cloud.google.com/blog/products/identity-security/10-questions-to-help-boards-safely-maximize-cloud-opportunities

207 UK National Audit Office. (2024, September). *Guidance for Audit Committees on Cloud Services.* https://www.nao.org.uk/wp-content/uploads/2021/04/guidance-for-audit-committees-on-cloud-services-2024.pdf

208 Pirchalski, E., Herndon, B. (2024, December 11). *Tuning Corporate Governance for AI Adoption.* NACD. https://www.nacdonline.org/all-governance/governance-resources/governance-research/outlook-and-challenges/2025-governance-outlook/tuning-corporate-governance-for-ai-adoption/

209 Giunta, T., Suvanto, L. (2024, September 17). *Board Oversight of AI.* Harvard Law School Forum on Corporate Governance. https://corpgov.law.harvard.edu/2024/09/17/board-oversight-of-ai/

210 *Nonprofit Fiduciary Duty + Responsibilities.* (2024, December 12). BoardSource. https://boardsource.org/resources/fiduciary-responsibilities/

211 Wex Definitions Team. (n.d.). *Definition of Fiduciary Duty.* Cornell Law School, Legal Information Institute. https://www.law.cornell.edu/wex/fiduciary_duty

212 Palmer, J. (2022, December 1). *What is Duty of Care?* https://www.onboardmeetings.com/blog/duty-of-care/

213 Huber, C., Sukharevsky, A., & Zemmel, R. (2021, June 21). *5 Questions Boards Should Be Asking About Digital Transformation.* Harvard Business Review. https://hbr.org/2021/06/5-questions-boards-should-be-asking-about-digital-transformation

About the Authors

Meredith Stein, CPA, has substantial and diverse experience in the domain of governance, including designing, operationalizing, and assessing governance structures, including ERM, COSO / internal controls, and external audits of financial statements. As a public sector employee in the U.S. Federal Government, she organizes, aligns, assesses, remediates, and monitors corporate and program risk to ensure program integrity and compliance. Meredith also participates in governance-related learning and development initiatives.

She was a manager at KPMG, conducting audits and leading Sarbanes-Oxley and governance consulting projects. Meredith is also a board member serving on committees for two non-profit organizations. Meredith received her degree in Accounting from the American University Kogod School of Business.

With over 30 years of experience in enterprise technology, **David S. Linthicum** is a globally recognized thought leader, innovator, and influencer in cloud computing, AI, and cybersecurity. He is the author of over 17 best-selling books, over 7,000 articles, and over 100+ courses on LinkedIn Learning. He is also a frequent keynote speaker, podcast host, and media contributor on topics related to digital transformation, cloud architecture, AI, and cloud security.

He also drives new market offerings, service innovation, and thought leadership outreach, leveraging his extensive knowledge and experience in generative AI and cloud computing for business agility and growth. David is passionate about educating and empowering the next generation of cloud professionals, as he serves as an adjunct instructor for Louisiana State University and a mentor.

List of Figures

Figure 1.1 Cloud Governance House: A Perspective on the Cloud Governance Ecosystem —— 7

Figure 3.1 The Cloud Enabled-AI —— 24

Figure 5.1 CIO Role, by Decade —— 61

Figure 6.1 Extended-Enterprise: Web of Data Sharing in the Cloud Computing Domain —— 68

List of Tables

Table 1.1   Examples of Utopian Promises of the Cloud —— 4
Table 1.2   Top 25 List of the Chaotic Realities of the Cloud —— 5
Table 1.3   Definition of Cloud Governance —— 7
Table 1.4   Variables of TOE Context Framework to Limit Chaos —— 8
Table 1.5   Example Use Cases for Quantum Computing —— 10
Table 2.1   Summary of the Cyber-Attack on Ticketmaster —— 17
Table 2.2   Summary of the Cyber-Attack on Solar Winds —— 18
Table 2.3   Summary of the Cyber-Attack on Blackbaud —— 19
Table 3.1   Definitions of Cloud Computing – Selected Examples —— 22
Table 3.2   Artificial Intelligence Technologies —— 23
Table 3.3   Three Major Cloud Service Models —— 24
Table 3.4   Cloud Computing Deployment Models —— 26
Table 3.5   Categories of Cloud Vendors —— 27
Table 3.6   Descriptions of Vendor Selection Criteria —— 28
Table 4.1   Framework for Developing a Cloud Strategic Plan —— 37
Table 4.2   Top 25 List of the Impact of Not Having a Cloud Strategic Plan —— 39
Table 4.3   Enablers of Cloud Strategy – Selected Examples —— 40
Table 4.4   Examples of Cloud Service Objectives and KPIs —— 41
Table 4.5   Examples of Reliability and Availability Service-Level Targets —— 42
Table 4.6   Levels of a Maturity Model —— 44
Table 4.7   Financial Governance Measures —— 45
Table 4.8   Comparison of the Benefits of On-Premises Versus Cloud Environment —— 46
Table 4.9   Options for Legacy Technology in Cloud Migration —— 48
Table 5.1   Definitions of Adaptive and Transformation Change —— 49
Table 5.2   Options for Addressing Gaps in Cloud Skill – Selected Examples —— 54
Table 5.3   Overview of the ACADEMIES Framework —— 56
Table 5.4   AI and Cloud L&D Program Topics —— 58
Table 6.1   Stakeholders of a Cloud Shared Responsibility Model —— 66
Table 6.2   List of Cloud Computing Risks —— 69
Table 6.3   Commonly Used Techniques to Identify Risk —— 73
Table 6.4   Example ERM Portfolio —— 74
Table 6.5   Examples of ERM Responsibilities —— 78
Table 6.6   CSA CCM: Cloud Control Domains —— 80
Table 7.1   Summary of Cybersecurity Frameworks Available in the Public Domain —— 83
Table 7.2   Components of the U.S. NIST Cybersecurity Framework —— 84
Table 7.3   Examples of Security Threats Unique to the Cloud —— 85
Table 7.4   Example AI-Enabled Cloud Security Technologies —— 87
Table 7.5   Cloud IR Framework —— 88
Table 7.6   Key Aspects about Cloud IR —— 90
Table 7.7   Benefits and Challenges of Adopting a Zero Trust Approach —— 92
Table 7.8   Cloud Security Domains —— 93
Table 8.1   Three Levels of Compliance of the EU Cloud of Conduct —— 98
Table 8.2   Example Compliance Best Practices —— 99

Table 8.3   Examples of Laws, Regulations and Guidelines with Cloud Implications —— **100**
Table 8.4   Essential Elements of Compliance and Ethics Programs —— **103**
Table 8.5   Primary Security Services Provided by CASBs —— **105**
Table 9.1   Examples of How Internal Audit Can Leverage AI —— **108**
Table 9.2   Overview of AICPA-SOC for Service Organization Frameworks —— **110**
Table 9.3   Examples of ENISA Cloud Assurance Frameworks —— **111**
Table 9.4   Examples of ISACA Cloud Assurance Frameworks —— **112**
Table 10.1   Actions to Strengthen Board Oversight —— **115**
Table 10.2   Questions from the Board on Cloud Governance —— **116**
Table 10.3   Questions from the Audit Committee on Cloud Governance —— **117**
Table 10.4   Questions from the Board on AI Governance —— **118**
Table 10.5   Perspectives on Fiduciary Responsibilities of US Boards —— **120**
Table 10.6   Questions Management Should Ask to Assess Member Preparedness —— **121**

List of Boxes

Box 1.1 Edge computing enables IoT —— 14
Box 1.2 Cloud Governance Success Story —— 15
Box 3.1 Who is Responsible for Managing a Cloud Inventory —— 32
Box 4.1 Capability Maturity Model —— 43
Box 4.2 Financial Governance —— 45
Box 4.3 Managing Cloud Performance —— 46
Box 4.4 Legacy System Migration Decisions —— 46
Box 5.1 Role of the CIO —— 60
Box 6.1 Risk Identification Techniques —— 73
Box 6.2 Illustration of a Cloud and AI ERM Portfolio —— 74
Box 6.3 Examples of ERM Responsibilities —— 78
Box 6.4 CSA CCM domains —— 80
Box 7.1 CSA's Cloud Security Domains —— 93
Box 10.1 Fiduciary Duties —— 119

Index

Agentic AI 11–12, 51, 57, 75
Architecture 14, 38, 42, 54, 58, 90
Artificial Intelligence (AI) 9, 11, 13–17, 19–25, 28, 36, 54, 74–78, 86–87, 100, 102, 118–119
Asset discovery tools 31, 105–106
Audit committee 79, 117–118
Augmented Reality (AR) 58

Big data 9, 13–14
Board of Directors 114–121
Budget considerations 42, 59, 72, 92, 106, 112

Capability Maturity Model 43–44
Carbon 4, 16, 20–21
CCoE 32, 38, 40, 44, 51, 60
Change management 5, 8, 15, 39, 49–60, 69, 93, 117
Chief Audit Executive (CAE) 79
Chief Executive Officer (CEO) 75, 77–78
Chief Financial Officer (CFO) 36, 77–79
Chief Information Officer (CIO) 36, 43, 50, 60–61, 74–79
Chief Risk Officer (CRO) 79
Cloud Access Security Broker (CASB) 105
Cloud
– adoption 5, 15, 32, 36, 39–40, 42, 48–51, 53–54, 59–60, 69, 114, 116–117
– asset inventory 5, 15, 22, 30–32, 39, 44, 70, 76–77
– breach 5, 16–20, 28, 39, 65, 69–71, 76, 81, 87, 92, 94
– Center of Excellence 32, 38, 40, 44, 51, 60
– cost 15, 39, 41, 45–46, 53–54, 77, 79, 92
– gaming 12
– laws and regulations 96–103
– migration plan 36, 40, 46, 48, 117
– misconfigurations 41, 69, 86, 97, 108
– performance management 35, 40–42, 46, 57
– skills 9, 11, 13, 15, 37, 44, 49, 51, 53–55, 58, 60, 69–70, 115–117
– sprawl 30
– strategy 35–37
Cloud Controls Matrix (CCM) 71, 80–81, 84. See also Cloud Security Alliance

Cloud Governance House 7–8
Cloud Security Alliance (CSA) 28, 35, 67–68, 71, 80, 84, 86, 88–90, 105. See also Cloud Controls Matrix
Cloud Service Provider (CSP) 5, 9, 13, 20–21, 24–32, 37–39, 42, 44–47, 50, 53, 55, 65–70, 72–74, 77–79, 88–91, 97–98, 102, 104–105, 107, 111, 113, 117
COBIT 83, 103, 112
Community cloud 26
Compliance 96, 98, 102–105
Concentration risk 5, 39, 77, 117
Cyber-attacks 16–20, 91
Cyber insurance 5, 39, 71, 76
Cyber resilience 12, 65, 76–77, 80, 85, 91, 107, 111, 114, 119

Data breach 5, 16–20, 28, 39, 65, 69–71, 76, 81, 87, 92
Data center 14, 20–21, 26, 37–38, 54, 90
Data ethics 8, 23
Data governance 28, 69
Data sovereignty 12, 27
Deep learning 23–24
Democratization IT 4, 50, 66
Deployment models 22, 25–26, 28, 72, 90, 98
Digital skill gap 13, 51, 53–55, 60

Ecosystem 6–7, 13, 26–27, 38
Edge computing 9, 14, 26, 91
Emissions 16, 20–21
Enterprise risk management (ERM) 66, 71–74, 80, 94
European Network and Information Security Agency (ENISA) 22, 73, 83, 111
Exit strategy 29, 38, 46, 69, 117
Expense 45, 69, 71, 76, 106
Extended enterprise 5, 39, 66–68
External audit 79, 109, 113

Fiduciary duties 21, 115, 119–120
Financial governance 45, 71, 76, 106
FinOps 15
Fit for purpose 115–116

https://doi.org/10.1515/9783111617459-016

General Data Protection Regulation (GDPR)
51, 97, 100, 104–105
Generative AI 5, 13, 15, 20, 23–25, 39, 47, 50–51,
58, 70, 102

Healthcare 11, 14, 25–26, 92, 99–100
Health Insurance Portability and Accountability
Act (HIPAA) 101, 105
Hybrid cloud 12, 26–27, 37, 47, 68, 86, 91–92, 94,
98, 106, 112
Hyperscalers 26–27, 67

Incident response 5, 8, 39, 44, 70, 79, 81–82,
87–94, 119
Industry cloud 26
Internal audit 36, 50, 78–79, 107–108, 112–113
Internet of Things (IoT) 9, 12–14, 23, 57, 83, 95

Key Performance Indicators (KPIs) 40–41, 44, 57

Learning & Development (L&D) 55–58
Legacy 4, 8, 15, 35–36, 43, 46, 48, 92, 117

Machine learning 23–24, 82, 107–108
Malware 14, 16–19, 87–88, 105
Managed Service Providers (MSP) 27, 32, 45, 68
Microcloud 26
Multi-Cloud 26, 30, 37, 68, 72, 77, 87, 91–92,
98–99, 106, 112

National Institute of Standards and Technology
(NIST) 16, 22–26, 82–85, 89, 102

On-premises *vs.* cloud environment 40, 43,
46–48, 85, 97–98, 112
Ownership 29, 32, 37, 38, 47, 69, 77, 89

Public cloud 25–27, 37, 41, 47, 57, 68, 85–86,
91, 98

Quantum computing 4, 9–10, 13, 20, 25, 47, 87

Ransomware 5, 16, 18–19, 91, 105
Resilience *See* Cyber Resilience
Return on Investment (ROI) 4, 10, 43, 46, 53,
60, 70
Risk
– appetite 8, 77–78, 84, 116
– identification 69, 73–78
– management 7, 15, 32, 36, 65, 69–79, 83–84,
105, 110, 112, 114, 117
– mitigation 70–71, 73, 109, 119

Security technologies 19, 87
Service Level Agreements (SLAs) 5, 29, 31–32,
39, 46, 74, 77–78, 90, 104, 107, 113
Service Models 22, 24
Shadow IT 5, 39, 50, 66, 68, 85, 104–106
Shared responsibility model 8–9, 15, 26, 38, 44,
47, 50–51, 65–68, 71–74, 81, 89–91, 94,
97, 104
Sovereign cloud 26
Sprawl 30
Strategy 35–39
System and Organization Controls
(SOC) 109–111, 113

Vendor lock-in 29–30, 32, 77, 117

Water scarcity 16, 20–21, 47
Wicked problem 3, 6
Workforce 5, 8, 13, 36, 39, 47, 50–51, 53–55,
57–60, 92
Workloads 15, 21, 26, 30, 35, 37, 41, 44, 54, 67,
91, 94, 98

Zero Trust 82, 89–93

www.ingramcontent.com/pod-product-compliance
Lightning Source LLC
Chambersburg PA
CBHW071556200326
41519CB00021BB/6774